John Hn-late
1/5/2010

THE KEYS TO LEADING

Integrating Head With Heart

John Horan-Kates

authorHOUSE®

AuthorHouse™
1663 Liberty Drive, Suite 200
Bloomington, IN 47403
www.authorhouse.com
Phone: 1-800-839-8640

First published by AuthorHouse 11/29/2007

ISBN: 978-1-4343-3995-9 (sc)
ISBN: 978-1-4343-3996-6 (hc)

Library of Congress Control Number: 2007908448

Printed in the United States of America
Bloomington, Indiana

This book is printed on acid-free paper.

CONTENTS

PART I: FOUNDATIONS

PART II: JOURNALING ON CHARACTER

PART III: JOURNALING ON SKILLS

PART IV: JOURNALING ON RELATIONSHIPS

APPENDIX

ABOUT THE AUTHOR

"Above all else, guard your heart
for it is the wellspring of life."

Proverbs 4:23

INTRODUCTION

The purpose of this journal is to help leaders of all stripes link time-honored principles from respected exemplars together with our great wisdom and faith traditions to their leadership approach. This work continues to evolve from my own journey of "becoming" a leader.

Like most of us, my growth as a person and as a leader began at home. For me, that was in Detroit working various jobs to support my way through high school. It evolved through college and then grew quickly as a naval officer in Vietnam. Following military service, I settled into a career in the ski industry in Vail, Colorado and began what became an annual commitment to personal development seminars and workshops. These annual events evolved into a lifelong exploration, learning and growing as a leader while sharpening my own purpose as a builder of a spiritually-oriented community. And marriage and building a home and a family were woven in over the next twenty-five years.

Along the way, my wife Pam brought us back to our spiritual roots primarily to ensure our children had that foundation. It was during this period that several colleagues and I decided to launch an entity focused on personal leadership. That organization is now known as the Vail Leadership Institute and espouses a philosophy known as "inside-first." This approach focus on key principles of leading organized around three realms – character, skills and relationships. While there are many more principles, virtues, traits, etc. that can be drawn upon in affecting leadership, I have chosen here to limit the focus to ten principles that are essential to effective, ethical leadership. This whole concept is built around the notion that empowering leadership starts with one's character and that largely resides in the heart and emanates out from there.

But as this perspective was evolving, people kept asking me: "Why put so much emphasis on the heart when businesses say this is too soft. And why is character-driven leadership so important anyway?" Enron, Tyco and the other notable examples of corporate malfeasance addressed the first question by clearly showing something was amiss. These types of abuses are sprinkled throughout our history and will probably continue to occur because we haven't learned the lessons very well, and because we're often driven by flimsy values.

In terms of how good leadership is developed, for me, a spiritual perspective provided the best response to selfish and ego-centric behavior. Scripture had become an unyielding foundation upon which to build a leadership approach. It became solid rock such that I might be less likely to be tempted by current cultural influences.

The approach that is laid out in these pages has been distilled over a lifetime from lessons learned – both my own – and those of other successful and significant leaders and thinkers. But it's not just about what they have to say. It also involves what you have to say about these leadership concepts. Prompted by thought provoking questions, you will be asked to express what you think about a particular topic or issue. Writing out your thoughts and ideas is a very important leadership discipline. Being succinct and clear about a whole range of issues will help you develop and clarify your worldview. And this worldview then becomes part of your character. It will help you sharpen the most important leadership skill, and that is, to "know thyself."

Why should all of this be important to you? The answer lies in your potential. Leaders, particularly those emerging and developing in organizations, are the people who will make things better. Leadership may sound like some lofty concept for the really smart people, but the truth is, we're all leaders in one way or another. You are the leader of your life. And while your leadership will evolve, you're on the journey now. Take responsibility and make good choices.

My hope is that working through this little book, particularly the journaling weeks, will touch your life in a similar way that the writing of it has touched mine.

John Horan-Kates
Vail, Colorado
October 2007

"First cleanse the inside…
that the outside may be clean as well."

Jesus of Nazareth

ACKNOWLEDGEMENTS

There are a variety of people and sources that I have drawn upon in development of this journal. This thinking has evolved from numerous thought-leaders over many years. Many of them are described on the following page. This multiple thought-leader approach has morphed into an "open source" perspective, drawing upon the computer technology lingo that makes the philosophy "open" and available to all to build upon. This open source approach fosters the continued evolution of "inside-first" by allowing anyone to add to the philosophy and propose their thoughts for inclusion in the core thinking through a "wiki" on the Institute's web-site. This open source philosophy continues to this day and this book is part of my contribution.

Some of the numerous books and essays drawn upon from these thinkers are referenced following each chapter, in the Chapter Notes section, or more broadly in a Bibliography available at www.vailleadership.org/library. All of these influences, combined with Richard Leider's early suggestion to get in the habit of journaling one's thoughts, provided the impetus to start this work.

Credit also goes to Dann Coffey for his wonderful photography that honors the divine creation in nature.

Most importantly, credit goes to my wife, Pam, for standing by me all these years and for being the wonderful "prayer warrior" that she is.

Of course, beyond all earthly support, I'd be remiss in not acknowledging the inspiration I had in all of this that clearly came from above.

"Do you want to be a positive influence in the world? First, get your own life in order. Ground yourself in the single principle so that your behavior is wholesome and effective. If you do that, you will earn respect and powerful influence. Your behavior influences others through a ripple effect. A ripple effect works because everyone influences everyone else. Powerful people are powerful influences. If your life works, you influence your family. If your family works, your family influences your community. If your community works, your community influences the nation. If your nation works, your nation influences your world."

John Heider

Thought-Leaders

Many people have contributed to this work. Here are a few who stand out;

- **Richard Leider**: Founder of the Inventure Group; author of many books on purpose, particularly, "The Power of Purpose."

- **Frederic Hudson**, Ph.D.: Founder of the Hudson Institute; President of the Fielding Institute; author of "LifeLaunch."

- **Max DePree**: Former CEO of Herman Miller, Inc.; founder of the DePree Leadership Center; author of "Leadership as an Art."

- **Joseph Jaworski**: Founder of the American Leadership Forum; author of "Synchronicity – The Inner Path of Leadership."

- **Peter Vaill**, Ph.D.: Professor of Human Systems at George Washington University; Governor of the Center for Creative Leadership; author of "Learning as a Way of Being."

- **Sid Buzzell**, Ph.D.: Professor of Leadership Studies at Colorado Christian University; general editor of "The Leadership Bible."

- **David Burger**, Ph.D.: Adjunct Professor at the Center for Creative Leadership.

- **Peter Senge**, Ph.D.: Founder of the Society for Organizational Learning at MIT; author of "The Fifth Discipline."

- **Robert Greenleaf**: Founder of the Greenleaf Center for Servant Leadership; author of "On Becoming a Servant Leader."

- **Mathew Fox**, Ph.D.: Founder of the University of Creation Spirituality; author of the "Re-invention of Work."

- **Stephen Covey**, Ph.D.: Founder of the Covey Leadership Center; author of "Seven Habits of Highly Effective People."

- **Parker Palmer**, Ph.D.: Senior Advisor to the Fetzer Institute; author of "Let Your Life Speak" and "The Courage to Teach."

- **Bob Vanourek**: Retired CEO of Sensormatic, Inc.; Chairman Emeritus of the Vail Leadership Institute.

- **Larry Donnithorne**: President Emeritus of Colorado Christian University; author of "The West Point Way of Leadership."

- **John Heider**: Author of "The Tao of Leadership."

"Know thyself."

Plato

DEDICATION

This book is dedicated to the most important women in my life.
My mother, Bessie Virdin Kates.
My wife, Pam Horan-Kates
And my daughter, Brooke Horan-Kates

*"This is the true joy in life, the being
used for a purpose recognized by
yourself as a mighty one."*

George Bernard Shaw

FOREWORD

BY DR. LARRY R. DONNITHORNE

This journal can be life-changing. Not instantly. No, instant gratification is not the nature of meaningful life change. But if, despite that fact, you're still interested in real, deeply meaningful life change, read on.

That part of us where meaningful change occurs is often referred to as our character. Our character is a reflection of who we really are. On a coin, for example, the characters or markings on the coin identify it clearly – what nation minted it, what denomination of currency it represents, what value it has, etc. Likewise, your character reflects who you really are, deep down, and what value you have.

Your character is formed both consciously and subconsciously. Some events play upon you beyond your control and sculpt your character. But, at the same time, you can actually take steps to shape your own perspective for the better into a strong, positive character. Your own conscious choices of values and commitments to fundamental human principles also shape your character.

That is where the journal in your hands comes into play. John Horan-Kates has drawn together in one compact book the reflections of many years of experience – both his own experience and that of his colleagues and that of many admirable personalities of history. By engaging this journal conscientiously, you will be immersing yourself into the ways of thinking and feeling that have served men and women of strong, positive character over many centuries. You will be reflecting upon the virtues and life views revealed by exemplars like Jesus of Nazareth and etched in ancient, sacred texts, such as the Bible. You will be slowly absorbing into yourself the deep ideas that have drawn human society out of barbarism into civilization. Your character will be taking shape.

The character that will eventually have been shaped in you by the sculpturing effects of outside events and by your own conscious choices will, in due time, be clearly revealed. Your character will be uncovered in how you respond to the great trials, great opportunities, and great reversals that inevitably lie ahead in your future.

When those times come, what character will be revealed from within you? This book can be life-changing by helping you find those answers.

How to Use the
Journaling Chapters

It's really pretty straight forward. Each journaling chapter is organized around a key leadership principle, like "purpose," within the three realms of the "inside-first" framework; character, skills and relationships. Even though these three realms represent a understandable organizing model, it's important to realize that these principles are all interrelated and that effective leadership requires a comprehensive grounding - it's not just about skills. In a nutshell, the inside-first philosophy is often expressed as <u>leadership from the heart</u>.

Perhaps a few definitions of leadership would be helpful at this point. My preferred definition is "doing the right things for the right reasons." But there are many other relevant characterizations. For example, I appreciate "achieving good ends by right means" from Larry Donnithorne, President Emeritus of Colorado Christian University. And I particularly appreciate the humor of Robert Jarvik, the inventor of the first artificial heart, when he described leaders as, "visionaries with a poorly developed sense of fear and no concept of the odds against them." And I like Ken Blanchard's definition, which says; "Leadership is an influence process. Any time you are trying to influence the thoughts and actions of others toward goal accomplishment in either their personal or professional life you are engaging in leadership." [1]

I want to touch here on the value of writing, because it has been significant in sharpening my perspectives . I have found the discipline of organizing one's thoughts and ideas and getting them on paper to be challenging, but fulfilling. Pushing yourself to be succinct and clear is an important leadership skill. And it can therapeutic too. I appreciate Rick Warren's sentiment that "we remember what we record." [2]

The real meat of this work begins with "values" because values are the building blocks of leadership, especially in a spiritually-based approach. Stephen Covey describes values as internal, while principles are external. [3]

Even though the journaling is set around a five-day week, start each week on Sunday with the definition and overview of that week's key principle. Use that time to think about the week ahead, particularly with respect to the goals you want to accomplish. While the journaling is not intended to serve as a daily organizer, hopefully it will move you in the direction of being well organized.

The quotes and scripture references have been selected to relate to the principle of each day as well as a suggested "practice" noted as a sub-head. Each day's interpretation ends with a question intended to prompt your journaling. Use this space to reflect whatever comes to mind. Don't second guess yourself – write those thoughts down. Lastly, and importantly from a leadership perspective, note what action you feel called to take as a result of that day's journaling.

At the end of the week, go back and re-read that week's entries and make any additional notes that seem appropriate. Assess what you said you'd do. Also, if the principle reviewed that week grabbed you, check-out the additional references provided on the Review of the Week pages. Then on Sunday, start the process anew. Throughout the year, perhaps around the major holidays, go back and review your perspectives and commitments.

Two final notes on your approach. Get into the habit of journaling at a specific time each day. It is recommended that you choose between the early morning or early evening. I like the morning because starting in a reflective mode sets a positive tone for the day. I call it a "morning solo." Regardless, set aside a specific time. And then, most importantly, find time to pray that God's hand may be with you.

*"Let the morning
bring me word of your
unfailing love, for I have
put my trust in you."*

Psalm 143:8

PART I
FOUNDATIONS

The premise of this book is that effective, ethical leadership comes by integrating head and heart. It's not one or the other – but both – in a balance that produces desirable results. The "inside-first" approach advocates starting with the heart.

Regardless of what you're building, you've got to start with a foundation. This is the component that everything stands on. Long ago a man from Galilee advocated building on rock rather than sand.
And in leadership, the building blocks of that solid rock are values.

LEADERSHIP FRAMEWORK – VALUES

CHAPTER ONE

*"Leadership is an art, a performance art. And in the art of leadership, the
artist's instrument is the self.
The mastery of the art of leadership comes with the mastery of the self.
Ultimately, leadership development is a process of self-development."*

James Kouzes & Barry Posner

LEADERSHIP FRAMEWORK

EVOLUTION OF A LEADERSHIP FRAMEWORK

LEADERSHIP FROM THE HEART

In the recent literature on leadership, a focus on the inside is becoming more and more common. It's referenced in a variety of articles and books from Joe Jaworski's Synchronicity to Peter Senge's essay, "The Ecology of Leadership" to Bill George's book, True North. Sometimes you see it referenced as "inside-out" thinking; sometimes as the "inner" life. A whole special issue of the Harvard Business Review, sub-titled, "Why Knowing Yourself is the Best Strategy Now," talked about leadership being personal and put its focus on the inside. As a result, the heart-centered perspective is gaining momentum.

My own thinking solidified concurrently with the evolution of the Vail Leadership Institute's philosophy that ultimately led to coining the phrase "inside-first." This framework blends a practical approach with a holistic, heart-mind-spirit outlook that is very much needed in today's fast-paced world. At bottom, inside-first is about leading from a solid foundation.

The evolution of this philosophy continues to draw from a range of excellent theories, often referred to as a multiple thought-leader approach. In the process of developing this thinking, it became obvious how complex leadership can be with the wide variety of comprehensive approaches being taught and used. As a pragmatist, I felt the need to take a stab at simplifying things.

Thus the intent of this chapter is to outline this framework synthesized over many years. My purpose is to go beyond describing why inside-first thinking is important, and how it can be applied in the real world, to teeing-up the principles in the chapters that follow. But it's also an opportunity to tell a bit of my own story and how these principles have played a role in my evolution as a leader.

For me, it started in the late 60's with a stint in Vietnam as a naval officer. Living and working in crowded quarters taught me discipline, focus and organization. The long days and nights on the Me Kong River provided the opportunity for my first life plan and a vision of living and working in Colorado. And it launched the first step in my commitment to serving the nation.

By the mid-70's, I was living in Vail where my first exposure to structured leadership development came through the confrontational, but nevertheless valuable, est (Erhard Seminars Training) workshops. One of the significant take-aways was the commitment to periodically taking a look at my life to see if I was really making a difference. This willingness became an annual event, sometimes with my wife, sometimes on a business-sponsored retreat, but always in a reflective way. Regardless of form, this eagerness to learn opened the door to many thought-leaders and many perspectives.

Another lesson at this early stage was seeing the power of being personally responsible versus blaming others. As the Vice President of Marketing for Vail, I led a team of creative, energetic people who loved what they were doing in this spectacular mountain setting. But I struggled with some of the team when follow-through on our agreements was weak. I saw that I couldn't make them take action; I could only take responsibility for my half of the relationship. And in doing so, I could actually take 100% responsibility for myself and this allowed me to move away from the blame game. Experiencing this power of taking responsibility was life-altering.

Richard Leider was next in what would become a long line of influencers. His focus was purpose and he professed that to discover it, one must start on the inside with what's important, what we value, what we appreciate and where our talents and passions lie. Purpose, he contended, is one's reason for being. Early on in Vail, I felt drawn to help build the community and this would shape my next 30 years.

From the early-80's through the mid-90's, the influence of many thought-leaders served to plant seeds for a learning community of some kind. Clearly Stephen Covey made a significant impact, as did Scott Peck, Joe Jaworski, John Gardner, Peter Drucker and Robert Greenleaf. In his work as General Editor of The Leadership Bible, Sid Buzzell used a three-phased organizing structure that ultimately led to the adoption of the "water drop" as symbolic of this emerging perspective. This image, introduced by Buck Elliott, symbolized leadership emanating out from the center – from our inside.

But it was Leider's introduction in 1995 of Frederic Hudson, a delightful and sage psychologist-thinker-coach, that really helped launch a new course. Hudson's philosophy was based on a "cycle of renewal" that described how leaders are ever evolving through various phases and stages of life taking one both inside and then out. Sometimes we're in a phase when things are going well, when we're meeting our objectives and really producing the desired results. Sometimes we're in the "doldrums" when things seem out of synch or when we've got to let go of the past. As an evolving leader, I began to see how much I didn't know, and committed myself to the notion of lifelong learning. With Hudson's guidance, I became a leadership coach and learned the incredible power of questions.

Along the way, David Burger shared his "Natural Life Cycles" model, wherein he refers to the continuous seasonal nature of life reflected in the spring, summer, fall and winter cycles. Both the Burger and Hudson models are mirrored in what Colorado's Southern Ute Indians have called throughout their history the "Circle of Life" where our existence is a constant journey; where the cycles never end. Understanding these models caused me to develop our own "Seasons of Leadership" model. Thus it became more clear to me that, leadership, like life, was an evolving process.

It wasn't until later that thought-leaders like Peter Senge, Matthew Fox, John Heider, Bob Vanourek, Max DePree, Parker Palmer and Peter Block became influences. As I read the work of these masters, I began blending and synthesizing their philosophies with the teachings from a whole raft of biographies of people like Mother Teresa, Mahatma Gandhi, Theodore Roosevelt, Nelson Mandela, Winston Churchill, Abraham Lincoln, Ronald Reagan and others.

All great human achievement begins from within. Thus, inside-first leadership is a process that starts there. Inside is where we clarify our values and discover our purpose. Inside is where we develop character. Inside is where we store our convictions, our beliefs and our courage. These virtues within then guide us in our responsibilities through relationships with others. This approach allows people to better realize their leadership potential to make meaningful contributions to society.

The inside-first framework employs a continuous process that is always cycling and looping back. It's a flow from inside reflection to outside action with relationships as a constant backdrop. It's developed through a thoughtful process that helps people discover a deeper sense of themselves, their values, their beliefs and their purpose. And the thinking is fostered by a set of universal leadership principles and leading practices organized around character development, skillful actions and relationship building. A significant premise is that leadership engages us in others people's lives, and before inserting ourselves, all of us should know how to lead our own lives first.

Another way of saying this is that in order to grow as a leader one must first grow as a person. As a beginning point, this involves understanding our essence, integrating heart, mind and spirit, and then, with a focused inside and a commitment to serving others, we can attempt to lead. In this way, people sense our essence and will choose, voluntarily, to follow.

Developing one's inner capacity involves a number of perspectives that help leaders understand their essence. Central to this understanding is dialogue, a process that encourages us to engage others openly. It's an environment where small groups of leaders are comfortable interacting and sharing their stories, their deeper feelings and their concerns. Being receptive to these "respectful conversations," allowing the wisdom that naturally resides within a group of leaders, can be extremely powerful.

Some would tie it to our culture which is increasingly complex and fast-paced with globalization, technology, and more TV channels than we could ever imagine. And now, with terrorism close at hand, we have our safety to think about as well.

As the Enron-type scandals indicate, greed, materialism and destructive competition have some leaders, and often whole teams, moving in the questionable direction. Our litigious, cynical, hedonistic culture is producing many people who are largely self-absorbed and think of the common good as something for soft-headed monks. The media rationalizes its programming by saying they only sell what the public is buying while some leaders push to do whatever it takes because "it's just business."

If freedom and opportunity are going to spread in this world, we will need more from our leaders. The common good must be balanced with individual achievement and success. The head must become more integrated with the heart. The positive potential of people must be more fully developed.

WHAT DISTINGUISHES LEADING FROM THE INSIDE FIRST?

The inside is about heart - it's where character is built. Parker Palmer's perspective on the word heart is:

> *"In ancient times it meant that center in the human self where everything came together – where will and intellect and values and feeling and intuition and vision all converged. It meant the source of one's integrity."* [1]

We're working on the inside when we take that extra moment to reflect – to just be. The inner life is often about discovery, creativity and participation in the divine nature. In the Season's model, fall and winter are the "inside" seasons when we're harvesting, evaluating and sorting things out, preparing for our next phase. Palmer advocates attending to the inner voice through solitude, meditative reading, walking in the woods, keeping a journal or simply finding a friend who will listen.

The "outside" emanates mostly in the head; it's the doing part of life. If the inside tends to be more about renewal, the outside is more about information and action. For example, how we manifest spirituality is an outgrowth of that connection which we've developed largely in thoughtful reflection. Again, referring to the seasons, we're on the outside when we're in spring and summer, a time for planting, producing and achieving. Developing that strategic plan for reaching your sales goals clearly draws on outside skills.

As Palmer says in A Hidden Wholeness, "a person is healthy and whole when both the head and the heart are involved."[2] Perhaps the key differentiating feature of the inside-first approach is that it advocates a place to start – with the heart. The heart is significantly influenced by our individual spiritual perspectives, and when leaders acknowledge this side of themselves, they can tend to live more integrated, balanced lives. Palmer calls it living the "undivided life."

One of Stephen Covey's Seven Habits drawn from the prayer of St. Francis provides a great example here; "Seek first to understand, then to be understood." [3] Communication is a key skill that is a complex subject unto itself, but listening first before speaking reflects an approach with a touch more humility. After all, it's why God gave us two ears and only one mouth.

Gandhi typified this kind of leadership; he was a deeply spiritual man who spent many hours in reflection and meditation. But he was also a man of action. He didn't wait around to see who might follow; he simply moved on his convictions. When he launched his salt march to the sea it grew to overwhelming strength from the sheer volume of his followers.

For effective leaders, both parts are essential. We need to be both thoughtful and expressive; both sensitive and decisive. Both head *and* heart. Robert Greenleaf in his various writings on servant leadership references Jesus of Nazareth as an example of a leader who was both reflective and very much action oriented. With the phrase, "First cleanse the inside…that the outside may be clean also" [4] he summarized it well.

HOW CAN ONE VISUALIZE THIS THINKING?

The waterdrop image below portrays the radiating flow of the inside-first philosophy. It identifies values and beliefs as key to our leadership "foundation", "character" as an inside realm that drives how we'll behave, "skills" as the primary outside activity and "relationships" that pervades all parts. To many, relationships are probably the most important realm of leadership simply because almost everything happens through people. Think of this image as a way of seeing the flow of leadership.

Foundation
Understanding what you stand for

Character
Defining how you'll act

Skills
Producing results

Relationships
Making progress through people

WHAT ARE THE UNIVERSAL PRINCIPLES AND LEADING PRACTICES?

A pragmatist might say, "this is interesting stuff, but how do I put it into practice?" Within these major domains or realms, a set of universal principles and leading practices has emerged. Practices grow from a belief that focusing on application is central to effective leadership.

In this framework, before principles come values. Values underlie everything and are key drivers of much of our thought and behavior. Values are those virtues that we supremely treasure; those standards, beliefs and qualities we consider worthwhile and desirable. They serve as a guide for determining our individual worldviews. Most of us know inherently what we value, but it's amazing how few people have ever written them down. I've managed to narrow my core values down to five; faith, trust, action, education and community. Chapter 2 will go into some depth with values.

The full inside-first framework encompasses numerous principles, but for this book I have narrowed it down to the just the critical "keys," highlighted in the following charts. Because leadership is such a complex subject, I wanted to bring focus, first to those principles without which an effective, ethical leader cannot succeed.

With values as the foundational building blocks, the principles in the "character" realm help us distinguish our identity and articulate what we really stand for. Character development is not a quick-fix activity nor shaped by some intellectual approach. Rather, it's a long-term nurturing process blending experience, perspective and commitment. For most, it started at home and developed over time in the crucible of life. Congressman J.C. Watt says, "Character is how we act when no one is watching." [5]

The key principles in the character domain are purpose, integrity, attitude and commitment. Each of us might add other principles to this list that are important, but for simplicity sake, these are central to the inside-first framework. The charts that follow also display a single practice that one might find valuable. You can participate in the open source process by adding your own practices through the Institute's "wiki" at www.vailleadership.org/wiki.

PRINCIPLE	PRACTICE
Purpose	Develop your strengths and talents
Integrity	Walk your talk
Attitude	Take courageous but calculated risks
Commitment	Deliver on your promises in spite of your fears

Perhaps further definition of these key principles will help bring clarity to this framework. Journaling in the subsequent chapters will help draw out your own perspectives on these principles and their related practices.

Purpose is one of those universal principles that has both inside and outside dimensions. Quite simply, it's a quality around which you shape your life. An outside dimension of purpose is one's calling, a way of actively contributing to your world. Think of your calling as a response to an inner summons; as an assessment of what you want to accomplish.

My purpose is "building spiritually-oriented communities," an expression that evolved over many years. Building is what I do. First it was my home, then I helped build organizations that hopefully became institutions. And as I reflected on my purpose, I was reminded of my desire to avoid the nomadic lifestyle I saw in so many others, to put down roots in Colorado, and allow my kids to grow up in the same house. This passion influenced the "community" aspect of my purpose.

Integrity shouldn't need a great deal of explanation, but for some corporate leaders today, it has slipped away. It's an open question whether the Enron situation was an anomaly or more commonplace. And it's interesting how people can compartmentalize their behaviors and bend their values between work and home – basically living a divided life. We need more ethical leaders who strive for consistency between what they believe and what they actually do.

For me, integrity became a very real principle in the mid-80's when my bosses wanted to completely negate a legally binding contract. Even my willingness to re-negotiate wasn't enough. They said, "we're doing it our way - period." I couldn't work in that kind of environment so I gave up a dream job. To me, a deal is a deal – you don't break your word. This was about integrity. It was a sad day, but ultimately the right decision. In retrospect, I see now that their willingness to break the agreement was fueled in part by my arrogance. If my spiritual perspective had been further developed at the time, I might have seen my self-centered tendencies and been led differently.

Attitude is that critical quality that emanates from within and helps determine how we look at life. It's a series of choices we constantly make. Our attitude encompasses things like courage, humility and enthusiasm. When we're comfortable with what we stand for, then our attitude is much more likely to be positive. Attitude is often reflected in how full we see the glass.

Commitment is a state of being emotionally or intellectually bound to a course of action or person; keeping our word, regardless of the payback. These are powerful words and there's not a lot of wiggle room in them.

To some, a commitment is a promise that people can count on. To others, it's either a loose expression of what they'd like to see happen, or a statement that lacks real meaning. These kinds of statements might be made when a commitment is being sought, but if something better comes along, the deal is off. Too often our commitments can be shallow, without real intent to follow through. We say yes quickly, and then it hits us what that might mean. To understand further what your commitments mean, look at what it costs you to maintain your promises – what do you gain and what do you lose?

My strongest commitment is to my wife of 30 years. And while our marriage vows are binding enough, I promised my mother I would be married only one time. That commitment grew out of the anguish our family experienced from her divorcing my father. Out of this experience, I've held my commitments in business and personal life as sacred. It's central to who I am.

WHAT ARE THE CRITICAL LEADERSHIP SKILLS?

The second domain contains strategic "skills," principles and related practices that we use out in the world. These are principles with an action-orientation that move things and people forward toward producing results. To be effective, one must move beyond simply having good character to doing something with it. This realm might be labeled "skillful actions" and includes principles like visioning, communicating, learning and executing. There are obviously other valuable skills, but again, in an effort to simplify, the most important are highlighted here.

SKILLS

PRINCIPLE	PRACTICE
Visioning	Know where you want to be
Communicating	Listen fully with the intent to understand
Learning	Be a life-long learner
Executing	Foster a discipline of effective action

Visioning is an essential and extremely valuable leadership principle. Leaders see what others don't. They look for what is coming next. And while visioning is a skill that helps us paint vivid pictures, for it to be significant, it requires having an executable strategy that evolves in relationship with others.

My first experience with visioning took place in Vietnam aboard the USS Jennings County. Being isolated aboard a ship afloat in the Me Kong River gave me plenty of time to contemplate my future. Having skied in Vail and Aspen on way to catch my flight to Saigon, I was enamored of the mountains. I concluded right there in Southeast Asia, and wrote it down, that my vision of using my marketing degree and my love of skiing should unfold in Vail. It took me five years from that moment to land in Vail in 1974. In 1977, I was named Vice President of Marketing.

Communicating one's thoughts and ideas is surely a critical leadership skill. But even more important, is to seek understanding by listening. This principle is rooted in the notion that we don't, and can't, know everything. But by opening ourselves as learners, we can advance what we do know. As a two-way street, communicating is the beginning of understanding. Suzanne Maxwell, a communications consultant from Albuquerque, taught me and others in the Vail community what it meant to really listen. She introduced "dialogue" as a process to help community leaders slow down for a few moments to simply try to understand one another - rather than trying to win the conversation. This process puts a premium on listening, and as part of taking in others perspectives, shows that when we avoid interrupting, we have a chance of a better understanding.

Learning may not be at the top of everyone's list, but it represents an approach in our networked world that helps us to develop a more humble perspective. Learning as leaders is much less about formal education and more about thoughtful reading, participating, teaching and guiding others. And the power of the question cannot be over emphasized. Ron Heifetz of Harvard talks about "adaptive" skills where learning, and becoming expert in the management of processes, is central to advanced leadership.

Parker Palmer promotes a counterculture learning approach he calls "circles of trust," usually small groups that gather on a weekly, monthly, or even quarterly basis. These circles of trust can seem risky because they make us vulnerable. He says that our tendency is to "seek safety in abstractions, speaking to each other about our opinions, ideas, and beliefs rather than about what's really going on in our lives." [6] Palmer claims we tend to hide our true identities from each other and hide our beliefs from those who disagree with us to avoid conflict, challenge and change. Being open and honest is how real personal growth occurs and how our deepest challenges can be addressed.

My small group of four guys meets every Friday morning for at least an hour and a half. This is a "no agenda" group that meets around our shared Christian faith and agrees simply to love one another and avoid judging. We have wrestled with every conceivable business or personal issue, and in our circle of trust, we have helped one another through difficult ethical dilemmas. We wisdom of this group makes it one of my most powerful learning experiences.

Executing is simply the discipline of producing the desired results. It's the process of managing action; clarifying who's going to do what by when. Executing makes all the difference because it closes the gap between promises and results. However you want to refer to it – initiating, following-up, discipline, implementation, action – executing is relatively straight-forward stuff. It's the blocking and tackling of leadership. And while it may sound simple, it's definitely not easy.

HOW DOES RELATIONSHIP-BUILDING FIT?

The "relationship" domain recognizes that leaders generally get things done with and through others. Sometimes leadership may seem straight-forward, but things tend to get a little complicated when we involve others. Human nature adds all the complexity we could ever want. So a focus on relationships is central to "inside-first" leadership. Here we look at the principles of serving, love and spirituality.

PRINCIPLE	PRACTICE
Serving	Help others become successful
Love	Live the Golden Rule
Spirituality	Know your God and deepen your faith

Serving is a principle about which Robert Greenleaf was prolific. His test for servant leadership was "do those served grow?" Serving is other-centered versus self-centered. It's helping others become successful by giving-up control. Serving is having the courage to act and letting your example be the message. Joe Jaworski commented that "the deeper territory of leadership is collectively listening to what is wanting to emerge and having the courage to do what is required." [7] The serving perspective recognizes that power is granted to the leader by followers. It's a hard concept for the autocratic generation to embrace, but as technology spreads, more control will flow from individuals at the bottom.

My first experience with serving occurred when I volunteered for Navy Officer Candidate School in 1967. In the midst of growing protests on college campuses against the war in Vietnam, I just felt that my duty was to serve. In my view, it was not a time to question but to step-up. As it turned out, serving our country became a real turning point in my life. I experienced that freedom is not free, but it is worth living and dying for. It clearly instilled a deep patriotic spirit in my soul and is the reason I well-up whenever I hear the National Anthem.

Love is a soft concept – too soft for many corporate executives. But love is the key to good relationships. And getting things done through others is central to leadership. Love is about respect and kindness.

It's about the Golden Rule. It's the appeal to "love your neighbor as yourself."

In a comprehensive article in <u>Fast Company</u> magazine about technology entrepreneurs, Tim Sanders claimed that "The most powerful force in business is love. It's what will help your company grow and become stronger. It's what will propel your career forward. It's what will give you a sense of meaning and satisfaction in your job, which will help you do your best work." [8]

Spirituality can mean many things to many people. One way to think of it is as an orientation to a higher power beyond ourselves, what I call God, without aligning directly to a specific religious doctrine. Peter Block calls spirituality "the process of living out a set of deeply held personal values, of honoring a presence greater than ourselves." [9]

The theologian Matthew Fox defines spirituality as "the constant expansion of divine potential."[10] One might posit that spirituality resides inside, in one's heart, and so logically thought of as a character trait. Others may see it more as a relationship with that higher power. Either way, spirituality is a principle that is central to effective leadership in the twenty-first century. The primary reason is that if we want to change behavior, the best approach is to change hearts. And the best way to change hearts is to recognize, as Rick Warren says in the opening line of his wildly successful book, <u>The Purpose Driven Life</u>, "it's not about you." [11] So when we acknowledge that higher power, we can begin to get beyond ourselves and grasp the value of others.

My spiritual perspective deepened one night in 2005 when I heard from God at 2:30 in the morning. I call it my Holy Spirit moment when the words "declare your faith – stay the course" had me straight-up in bed, totally wide awake. I jumped out of bed to write down these words and spent the next year sorting out their meaning. Writing this journal became the declaration part as I expressed my values and beliefs in these pages.

The "stay the course" part was less clear at first. Did it mean simply to keep doing professionally what I was doing? About a year later, a second "bolt of lightning" came that said "I will show you the way - look for the open door." With this, I began to realize that God's got a plan for my life and work, and my job is to trying to discern that plan by walking through those open doors.

AND SO, IN SUMMARY...

This list of universal principles has been distilled and synthesized from a wide variety of people and sources over many years. But without practices, these principles might be viewed simply as intellectual concepts. Practices help us see how we can apply these principles in the real world. The leading practices identified above with each principle are only intended to be single examples of the "inside-first" approach. Add those practices that resonate with you as you think about this philosophy.

Leadership can be complex and multi-faceted. As a contrast, the "inside-first" framework is a simple and pragmatic way of looking at the most important aspects of leadership...and our lives. To be effective, to produce the desired results, we need to hone the inside first. And since leadership evolves, think of this as a point of departure !

CHAPTER TWO

"The skin wrinkles. The hair turns white. The days become years, but important things don't change."

Mother Teresa

VALUES

Values

Building Blocks for Leaders

Some say leadership is complex, and from many perspectives it is. But it can also be quite straight-forward when viewed from the standpoint of what's really important. A close look at your core values can be very helpful, because an "inside-first" framework advocates that values, particularly spiritually-oriented values, inform your ethical standards, and they in turn define your character.

A good way of looking at the distinction between values and principles is Stephen Covey's perspective that "values are internal and principles are external." [1] Values serve as a guide for what you supremely treasure. Principles are those tenets that you act upon. In his book True North, Bill George says, "Principles are values translated into action." [2]

As an example, "community" is a value that many people hold – it's a quality that they feel has been lost and want it back in their lives. But, community is not really something that you do. On the other hand, "serving" is a principle that takes action on that community value. Serving is something you do – it's external. So, we hold values but act on principles.

The Institute defines values as the building blocks that you feel are vitally important - those qualities that live in your heart and form the base for your decision-making. They govern most of your thoughts, attitudes and behavior. And interestingly, they don't really change very much.

Ethics, a critical leadership issue, is the code of values which guide your actions. This code is sometimes referred to as your ethical compass. While there are many descriptions of ethics in leadership, one of the best comes from Bill Grace of the Center for Ethical Leadership in Seattle. He defines ethical leadership as "knowing your core values and having the courage to act on them…" [3]

Why is it so important to understand your values? Why do so many leadership experts start here? The answer lies in the fact that values are the basis of an ethical life. Underneath all of your feelings, perspectives and actions lie values. Values serve as a guide and they describe what you stand for. As an example, one person might choose "family" as a core value, while for someone else "nature" might be a broader value they draw from. These are both legitimate values and their centrality in your life depends on your perspective.

"Each time a man stands up for an ideal, or acts to improve the lot of others or strikes out against injustice, he sends forth a tiny ripple of hope…"

Robert F. Kennedy

If values guide your actions, what then determines your values? Most psychologists would say we all have a "value-system" shaped in part by our family, friends and influenced through all the school years by the culture of the time, and lastly, by our spiritual perspective. You can tell what you value by how you spend your resources - your time, your talents and your money.

Your value-system matures as these early influences take their effect and blend with experience. Values can vary widely from the more passive, like beauty and joy, to the more worldly, like success and money. Many leadership experts talk about "universal values" that are subscribed to by most of the wisdom and faith traditions. Their lists typically include values like love, peace, happiness, freedom and justice, among others. The creator gave us free will to choose the values we cherish. And for all of us, making these choices is both a right and a responsibility.

Another way of understanding these concepts is to look at them as a whole – as in your worldview. Chuck Colson, in his book <u>Being the Body</u>, describes a worldview as a "set of suppositions that each person holds about how the world works and how we fit into it." [4] Colson makes a strong case for a "biblical" worldview that bases one's life on scripture and the values that were advocated by the patriarchs, the prophets as well as by Jesus of Nazareth.

A worldview might be thought of as a filter on the lens through which you see things. It's a comprehensive perspective from all of those values and virtues that you've come to draw upon most regularly. It might include perspectives on politics, economics, ethics, the environment, spirituality, personal development and learning. In its fullest, your worldview might touch on the questions like; "What is the origin and meaning of life?" or "Who or what is at the center of your being?"

Spiritually-oriented leaders draw upon many of the great wisdom and faith traditions as the foundation for their lives. Throughout the Torah, the Old and New Testaments, in the Koran, in the Bhagavad Gita, divine inspiration moved the various writers to share stories and insights that can guide us in every aspect of leadership.

"Every man gives his life for what he believes. Every woman gives her life for what she believes. Sometimes people believe in very little or nothing, and yet they give their lives to that little or nothing. One life is all we have and we live it as we believe in living it and then it's gone. But to surrender what you are and to love without belief is more terrible than dying – even more terrible than dying young."

Joan of Arc

The process of defining your core values can take some time. It involves identifying and weighing worldly values versus spiritual values; distinguishing primary values from those that are secondary. The approach here is to uncover what you actually value, not to advocate what you should value.

The following paragraphs are a sampling of words that speak to common values that many people recognize, organized into two primary groups. "Head" values tend to revolve around your capabilities, strengths and intelligence and are more outward. Your "heart" values lean more toward the emotional side, including things like feelings and relationships. Some values may seem more desirable than others, but we know that good leadership requires both head and heart. Living an optimal balance is the key.

As you review these words, consider highlighting or making a list of those core values that reflect what you stand for – what you base your leadership, and your life, on. These core values are the really important ones that you might die for.

Here's a list of sample "head" values. Add to it as you feel moved.

ACHIEVEMENT, ADVANCEMENT, ADVENTURE, AUTHORITY,
AUTOMONY, AMBITION, APPEARANCE, BALANCE, CANDOR,
CHALLENGE, COMPETITION, COMPETENCE, CREATIVITY,
COLLABORATION, COMMUNITY, CONTRIBUTION, CONSENSUS,
COOPERATION, DISCIPLINE, DUTY, EDUCATION, EQUALITY,
EXCELLENCE, FAIRNESS, GROWTH, HEALTH, HOME, HONESTY,
IMAGINATION, INDIVIDUALITY, INNOVATION, INVOLVEMENT,
INFLUENCE, KNOWLEDGE, LAWS, MONEY, NATURE, OBEDIENCE,
PERFECTION, POSITIVENESS, POWER, PRUDENCE, UNIQUENESS,
QUALITY, RECOGNITION, RELIGION, SECURITY, SIMPLICITY,
STATUS, SUCCESS, TEAMWORK, TRUTH, WEALTH, WINNING,
WORK AND VARIETY

And here's a list of some "heart" values. Again, add to it as necessary.

ABUNDANCE, ATTITUDE, ARTISTIC, AUTHENTICITY,
BEAUTY, CHARITY, COMPASSION, COURAGE,
EMPOWERMENT, FAITH, FAMILY, FORGIVENESS, FREEDOM,
FRIENDSHIP, GOODNESS, HAPPINESS, HOPE, HUMILITY, HUMOR,
JOY, JUSTICE, KINDNESS, LOVE, LOYALTY, MERCY, OPENNESS,
PASSION, PATIENCE, PEACE, PERSEVERANCE, RELATIONSHIPS,
SERVICE, SPIRITUALITY, STEWARDSHIP, RESPECT, RESILENCE,
TRANQUILITY, TRUSTWORTHINESS,
UNDERSTANDING AND WISDOM.

As our values become more clearly defined, we need to move from embracing them intellectually to acting on them consistently. One way to start is to understand why each value is important. Why do you want that specific characteristic in your life?

Another way to look at values is to understand those values that you specifically resist or have difficulty with. These may be values that are right for someone else, but they really don't resonate with you. For example, a value I resist is authority and my explanation is that I really don't like people telling me what to do.

Yet another approach is to think about those values you treasure the most and consider how you act those out on a day-to-day basis. How consistent are you? For example, do you strive to always tell the truth at home, yet bend the story at work because "everybody else does it?" Are you really committed to living in integrity with your values? In leadership, it's more about what you do than what you say, hence the most confirming way we describe our values is through our actions.

Some people refer to this as "walking your talk." Like the rudder of a ship, values serve to guide our course through life. You are aligned when you transform your values into actions. The famous phrase, "actions speak louder than words," helps you move from what you believe to how you behave. Regardless of where you are in your spiritual walk, this is the hard stuff.

Great leaders take the right actions for the right reasons. And spiritually-based leaders find guidance in divine inspiration. Before making important decisions, seek wise counsel. Ask the "why" questions. Reflect in solitude. Pray for guidance. Consult with those you trust. Then choose based on your values. And finally, communicate your decision by letting your actions speak. Knowing your core values is critical, but more importantly, are you really committed to living in integrity with those values? Are you willing to really walk your talk?

"What you do reveals what you believe."

Henry Blackaby

PART II
JOURNALING ON CHARACTER

With values as a foundation, the principles in the "character" realm
help us distinguish our identity and define how we'll act.
Character development is not a quick-fix activity nor shaped
by some intellectual process. Rather, it's a long-term
nurturing process blending experience
with matters of the heart.

In this section we begin to journal our thoughts around four of the
most important universal principles in character development.

PURPOSE – INTEGRITY
COMMITMENT – ATTITUDE

CHAPTER THREE

"The world needs people with the patience and the passion to make a pilgrimage not only for their own sake but also as a social and political act. The world still waits for the truth that will set us free – my truth, your truth, our truth – the truth that was seeded in the earth when each of us arrived here formed in the image of God. Cultivating that truth, I believe, is the authentic vocation of every human being."

Parker Palmer

PURPOSE

KEY PRINCIPLE THIS WEEK: PURPOSE

"Our deepest fear is not that we are inadequate. Our deepest fear is that we are powerful beyond measure. It is our light, not our darkness, that most frightens us. We ask ourselves, who am I to be brilliant, gorgeous, talented and fabulous? Actually, who are you not to be? You are a child of God. Your playing small doesn't serve the world. There is nothing enlightened about shrinking so that other people won't feel insecure around you. We are all meant to shine. It is not just in some of us, it's in everyone. And as we let our own light shine, we unconsciously give other people permission to do the same. As we are liberated from our own fear, our presence automatically liberates others."

Nelson Mandela

Purpose: *your reason for being; the principle around which you structure your life; a source of energy and direction; the answer to why you are here.*

Richard Leider, author of the Power of Purpose, says, "Purpose answers the question: what am I trying to do with my life? Purpose is that deepest dimension within us – our central core. Purpose is already within us waiting to be discovered." [1]

Purpose is clearly something beyond your job and encompasses thoughts bigger than your self-serving interests and desires. Your purpose is influenced most directly by the values and beliefs that you hold closest in your heart. It's not simply a goal; goals are something to be achieved. A purpose is much larger and represents the direction or underpinning for a meaningful life; it's why you get up in the morning.

Essence is another word that reflects on purpose. What is at the essence of your being or the fundamental nature of who you are? Rick Warren's extremely popular book, the Purpose Driven Life, brings focus to eternal purposes. This week we will examine purpose from the perspectives of your anthropology, your gifts, passions, callings, and ultimately, your legacy.

With "purpose," we begin the journaling sections of this book. Try to spend at least 10-15 minutes each day, either early in the morning or early in the evening, reflecting on the quotation, the commentary, the specific question posed, and lastly, the action that your thoughts urge you to take.

I Choose to Be Purposeful...

I will not wander aimlessly,
for my life is too valuable to squander.
I promise to develop my talents
to nurture my dreams
and to strive to understand
what God intends for my life.
I sense clarity here will not come easily,
but you can count on me
to shape a meaningful purpose for my life !

PURPOSE

KNOW YOUR HISTORY

> *"When I want to understand what is happening today*
> *or try to decide what will happen tomorrow I look back.*
> *A page of history is worth a volume of logic."*
> **Oliver Wendell Holmes**

Before moving ahead, it can be helpful to reflect back. A good way to begin the process of understanding your purpose is to know from where you've come – to know your own anthropology.

Most basically, know your heritage; your parents and grandparents and as far back as you are able to reach. If you were to trace your roots, what would you find? What languages, professions and faith traditions would you uncover? From your upbringing, what cultural and educational influences have stuck with you? The proverb that proclaims "the purposes of a man's heart are deep waters" asks you to look carefully into your background for clues and guidance as to your make-up. For example, your values and beliefs are the building blocks of your leadership approach and being clear about what is supremely important to you is central to setting meaningful goals.

You don't have to look back very far, but it can pay dividends!

Today's Journal

Over the years, who has most deeply influenced you? And why?

_____

_____

_____

_____

_____

_____

_____

_____

_____

_____

_____

_____

_____

_____

_____

_____

_____

_____

_____

Action Step – What one thing will you do today about these thoughts?

_____

_____

_____

PURPOSE

RECOGNIZE YOUR GIFTS

> *"We have different gifts, according to the grace given us. If a man's gift is*
> *prophesying, let him use it in proportion to his faith. If it is serving, let him*
> *serve; if it is teaching, let him teach; if it is encouraging, let him encourage;*
> *if it is contributing to the needs of others, let him give generously; if it is*
> *leadership, let him govern diligently;*
> *if it is showing mercy, let him do it cheerfully."*
> ### Romans 12:6-8

In this passage, the Apostle Paul describes the diverse gifts and talents needed to lead effectively. And he's also highlighting the fact that we have been endowed by our creator with different capabilities.

If you reflect back over time, your gifts and talents are probably pretty obvious. They are things that you find yourself naturally gravitating to. A talent is something you're most likely pretty good at. You don't have to brag about it because you just know it. You're probably exercising your God-given talents when you feel most energized and fulfilled.

Understanding and acknowledging your particular gifts, especially in the context of other talented people, and realizing that you probably can't do everything equally well, is a positive step in identifying your purpose.

Today's Journal

What is the primary gift God has given you?

_____

_____

_____

_____

_____

_____

_____

_____

_____

_____

_____

_____

_____

_____

_____

_____

_____

_____

_____

_____

Action Step – What one thing will you do today about these thoughts?

_____

_____

_____

_____

PURPOSE

FOLLOW YOUR PASSIONS

> _"Passions give life meaning, and it is through passionate commitment_
> _that we give our lives the particular meaning that they have."_
>
> **Tom Rollins**

Passion for a meaningful purpose is key for successful leaders. It's also usually central to living a happy, satisfied life. Passion comes from what you are attracted to - what you really pay attention to. For most great leaders, the motivation for that purpose comes naturally. It builds from what they are really devoted to and enthusiastic about.

Does your passion lean more toward physical activities, like sports or woodworking or more toward thoughtful pursuits, like writing, reading or music? Maybe it's other people – friends, family, children. Or perhaps you're an animal lover...horses, dogs - you name it.

Only you know...and you <u>do know</u> because you can feel it.

Today's Journal

What do you dream about? What do you lose yourself in?

_____

_____

_____

_____

_____

_____

_____

_____

_____

_____

_____

_____

_____

_____

_____

_____

_____

_____

_____

_____

Action Step – What one thing will you do today about these thoughts?

_____

_____

_____

_____

PURPOSE

Understand your Calling

> _"Vocation does not come from a voice 'out there' calling_
> _me to become something I am not._
> _It comes from a voice 'in here' calling me to be the person I was born to be,_
> _to fulfill the original selfhood given me at birth by God."_
>
> ### Parker Palmer

What is a calling and how do you know what's right for you? Webster refers to a calling as a career, a trade or a craft. Palmer uses the word vocation. While others might simply refer to it as your job, it's really more than that.

Richard Leider defines calling as our way of actively contributing in the world. He says, "Your calling fulfills your desire to use your gifts on things you feel passionate about."[2] A calling might be conveyed in a verb like building or teaching or writing or helping others – whatever you most love to do. Your unique calling draws upon those special gifts that you've been endowed with and that you regularly give to others. It's what you do !

Successful leaders find that there's real fulfillment in work that they enjoy – in work that relates directly to their calling. And these leaders continually refine their capacity - their skills - to realize their dreams. Understanding your calling helps on that longer journey toward fully realizing your purpose.

Today's Journal

What do you feel you've been called to do with your life?

_____

_____

_____

_____

_____

_____

_____

_____

_____

_____

_____

_____

_____

_____

_____

_____

_____

_____

_____

_____

Action Step – What one thing will you do today about these thoughts?

_____

_____

_____

_____

PURPOSE

"This is the true joy in life, the being used for a purpose recognized by yourself as a mighty one; the being thoroughly worn out before you are thrown on the scrap heap; the being a force of nature instead of a feverish, selfish little clod of ailments and grievances complaining that the world will not devote itself to making you happy. I am of the opinion that my life belongs to the whole community, and as long as I live, it is my privilege to do for it whatever I can. I want to be thoroughly used up when I die, for the harder I work, the more I live. I rejoice in life for its own sake. Life is no brief candle to me. It is sort of a splendid torch which I've got a hold of for the moment, and I want to make it burn as brightly as possible before handing it on to future generations. "

George Bernard Shaw

This is pretty lofty stuff - a purpose you call "mighty." How can you possibly look at things this way? Thinking about your legacy can give rise to what your purpose is today. Is your purpose meaningful and are you really making a contribution?

Working on a purpose can be inspiring because it answers the question; what am I trying to do with my life? It is clearly something beyond your career and encompasses thoughts bigger than your self-serving interests and desires. Regardless of where you are in your thinking on these issues, being specific about your direction, writing it down, will be very valuable. Your purpose and your goals will naturally evolve if you work at it!

For many leaders, leaving a legacy is often about appointing successors to continue the work – people who can reproduce or sustain the vision. Moses appointed Joshua to finish what he started. The legacy of the Man from Galilee remains because he carefully laid a foundation for his friends to carry on his work. Think of what lasting value you want to leave behind.

<u>*Today's Journal*</u>

What will your legacy be?

_____

_____

_____

_____

_____

_____

_____

_____

_____

_____

_____

_____

_____

_____

_____

_____

_____

_____

_____

_____

<u>*Action Step – What one thing will you do today about these thoughts?*</u>

_____

_____

_____

_____

PURPOSE

Take a moment to look back over your notes this week. Do your entries still resonate with you? Would you add anything?

And, how did you do on the actions steps you gave yourself? Be tough on yourself. If you didn't move on something, ask yourself why. And when you understand that "why", go just a little deeper and ask yourself again, why do you want that outcome.

Comment here with additional thoughts and with whatever else you need to do about your notes and actions.

_____

_____

_____

_____

_____

Here are a few references on "purpose" that might be helpful.

- **"The Power of Purpose: Creating Meaning in your Life & Work"** – Richard J. Leider

- **"Let Your Life Speak: Listening for the Voice of Vocation"** – Parker Palmer

- **"Man's Search for Meaning"** – Viktor Frankl

- **"The Eighth Habit: From Effectiveness to Greatness"** – Stephen R. Covey

- **"Answering Your Call: A Guide for Living Your Deepest Purpose"** – John P. Schuster

- **"The Purpose Driven Life"** – Rick Warren

"Don't ask yourself what the world needs. Ask yourself what makes you come alive, and go do that, because what the world needs is people who have come alive."

John Eldredge

CHAPTER FOUR

*"I hope I shall possess firmness and virtue enough to maintain
what I consider the most enviable of all titles, the character of an honest man."*

George Washington

INTEGRITY

KEY PRINCIPLE THIS WEEK: INTEGRITY

*"I use the word heart as they did in ancient times, when it didn't merely mean the emotions, as it tends to mean today. It meant that center in the human self where everything comes together –
where will and intellect and values and feeling and intuition and vision all converge.
It meant the source of one's integrity."*

Parker J. Palmer

Integrity: walking your talk; doing what you say you'll do; relates to your core beliefs in action.

Former Congressman J.C. Watts, described character as "what we do and how we behave when no one is watching." [1]   And integrity is one of the absolute key ingredients of character. It's much easier to act with integrity when the spotlight is on, but being trustworthy and honest because it is just the right thing to do is a statement of who you really are. A person with integrity will match his internal values with his external behavior. John Maxwell, in his book Ethics 101, defines integrity as "making your beliefs and actions line up." [2]

How do "ethics" and "morality" relate to integrity?   As the General Editor of The Leadership Bible, Sid Buzzell refers to ethics as a defined standard of right and wrong, while morality is a lived standard – what we actually do. To the extent that a person's ethics and behavior are integrated, that person has integrity. The opposite of integrity is hypocrisy.

But we're all human, and thus fallible and imperfect by nature. When a man of integrity stumbles, he makes it right.

I Choose Integrity...

I can tell the truth or I can fake it.
I can keep my promises
or change my mind when something better comes along.
But I cannot live that way, for my word is all I really have.
I thank the Almighty for giving me a humble heart,
and for showing me how to walk my talk.
I choose to live life with integrity.

INTEGRITY

WALK YOUR TALK

"You are already of consequence in the world if you are known as a man of strict integrity. If you can be absolutely relied upon; if when you say a thing is so, it is so; if when you say you will do a thing, you do it; then you carry with you a passport to universal esteem."

Grenville Kleiser

It seems so simple - just doing what you say you will. But as the saying goes, "It's easier said than done."

Of all the leadership principles, integrity makes almost everyone's list of most critical. Why is that? Most leaders would agree that integrity engenders trust and commitment and these results are key building blocks in the foundation of effective leadership.

Walking your talk simply means living those virtues or qualities that you say are important. If you say family is really important to you, then be there for them. If you talk about how you value being on time, then try being early every once in a while. Let your word be rock solid. Be reliable and dependable; don't waiver. And don't let your character be influenced by changing societal mores.

Today's Journal

Think of a time when you broke a promise. What did it cost you?

_____

_____

_____

_____

_____

_____

_____

_____

_____

_____

_____

_____

_____

_____

_____

_____

_____

_____

_____

_____

_____

Action Step – What one thing will you do today about these thoughts?

_____

_____

_____

_____

_____

INTEGRITY

Keep Your Word

> *"Lord, who may dwell in your sanctuary? Who may live on your holy hill?*
> *He whose walk is blameless and who does what is righteous, who speaks the*
> *truth from his heart...*
> *who keeps his oath even when it hurts."*
>
> ### Psalm 15:1-4

If you simply did what you said you would, wouldn't people generally start to trust you – to believe in you? On the contrary, if you consistently said one thing and did another, wouldn't people generally start to doubt you?

As leaders, we come across situations where we're challenged to live up to our commitments. When you don't keep your word, it's often because it isn't convenient or you rationalize a new course of action to minimize your losses. The reality is that sometimes circumstances change. When they do, that's the time to work toward a new agreement, not just walk away. When you can't secure that new understanding, do as the Psalmist says here - keep your oath even when it hurts.

Perhaps our society would be less litigious if we simply kept our word. Your "yes" should be good enough, but written agreements are often needed, not only to spell-out the details, but to hold people to their commitments. At a more personal level, what would your relationships be like if you said, "you can count on me," and then just delivered?

Today's Journal

If trust is built by keeping your word, what holds you back from standing firm on your commitments?

_____

_____

_____

_____

_____

_____

_____

_____

_____

_____

_____

_____

_____

_____

_____

_____

_____

_____

_____

Action Step – What one thing will you do today about these thoughts?

_____

_____

_____

_____

_____

INTEGRITY

Tell the Whole Truth

> *"For I imagine we are not striving merely to secure*
> *victory for my suggestions or for yours;*
> *rather we ought both of us to fight in support of the*
> *truth and the whole truth."*
>
> ### Socrates

Honesty produces trust. It seems so obvious, and yet, in many circumstances it seems so elusive. As the recipient of a communication, it seems natural to just want to know what's really going on. But as the sender, we often have the urge to stretch things.

As a leader, you're asked to communicate a great deal by telling a story or painting a vision. In doing so, you can easily succumb to expanding the truth just a little to look better. For example, you might stretch things by saying you were only going 60 MPH, when it was really 68. And then we say to ourselves, "hey, what's the big deal, I was pretty close." But we really stretched the truth - or more accurately, we lied. It sounds a little harsh, but that's the truth.

Interestingly, it's really easier to just tell the truth. You don't have to remember all the little white lies you told from one person to the next. And when you don't know the answer to even a simple question, what if we just said, "I don't know." What if we held ourselves to the standard of "the truth, the whole truth and nothing but the truth, so help me God?"

Today's Journal

What typically holds you back from telling the whole truth?

_____

_____

_____

_____

_____

_____

_____

_____

_____

_____

_____

_____

_____

_____

_____

_____

_____

_____

_____

Action Step – What one thing will you do today about these thoughts?

_____

_____

_____

_____

_____

INTEGRITY

FOLLOW THE GOLDEN RULE

> *"Asking the question, 'How would I like to be treated in this situation?'*
> *is an integrity guideline for any situation."*
>
> ### John C. Maxwell

It's a pretty simple concept to understand. Most people know the Golden Rule and believe it's valid. So what stands in the way of living and leading from this perspective?

As leaders, we're often faced with a fast paced life, lots of decisions and no small dose of stress. We're asked to move things forward...now. In these kinds of circumstances, too often we're not thinking of the people involved, but rather the project or the desired result. And very often our ego can come into play - we're thinking about what's best for us. Or what's most convenient.

The Golden Rule makes sense when we get beyond our own selfish needs. When we become "other-centered" we're more likely to ask Maxwell's important question. We just need to stop for a moment, and if we can focus our attention on how we'd like to be treated, it's easier to then move to how we might treat the other guy. We don't need a thick ethics manual to guide us. We just need this one little rule. Again, it's quite simple with the key being to get beyond yourself.

<u>*Today's Journal*</u>

When's the last time you clearly remember using the Golden Rule? What resulted?

_____

_____

_____

_____

_____

_____

_____

_____

_____

_____

_____

_____

_____

_____

_____

_____

_____

<u>*Action Step – What one thing will you do today about these thoughts?*</u>

_____

_____

_____

_____

_____

INTEGRITY

WHEN YOU STUMBLE, MAKE IT RIGHT

> *"Integrity doesn't demand perfection. Even the most
> morally committed people blow it.
> Integrity doesn't guarantee a perfect life, but it
> does require an integrated life.*
>
> **Sid Buzzell**

Integrity is such an important principle; it's hard too put too much emphasis on this virtue. It may be *the* cornerstone of effective, ethical leadership. It's all about doing what we say we will.

But leaders are imperfect creatures striving for perfection. So when you stumble, a critical step is to admit your mistake, recognize the impact of your failure and make it right. It's usually not that big of a deal, except we all struggle with admitting our mistakes. Apologize…say your sorry…clean-up your messes. Ask for forgiveness.

The moment you take this step, there can be sort of a freedom that comes over you. You don't have to hang-on tightly to being right. It's really OK. Fessing-up is about recognizing your humanity…and moving on.

Today's Journal

What was the hardest thing you ever had to apologize for, and what resulted?

_____

_____

_____

_____

_____

_____

_____

_____

_____

_____

_____

_____

_____

_____

_____

_____

_____

_____

Action Step – What one thing will you do today about these thoughts?

_____

_____

_____

_____

_____

_____

INTEGRITY

Take a moment to look back over your notes this week. Do your entries still resonate with you? Would you add anything?

And, how did you do on the actions steps you outlined? Be tough on yourself. If you didn't move on something, ask yourself why. And when you understand that "why", go just a little deeper and ask yourself again, why you want that outcome.

Comment here with additional thoughts and with whatever else you need to do about your notes and actions.

_____

_____

_____

_____

_____

Here are a few references on "integrity" that might be helpful.

- **"Ethics 101: What Every Leader Needs to Know"** – John C. Maxwell

- **"Leadership and the Inner Journey"** – Interview of Parker Palmer in <u>Leader to Leader</u> by L.J. Rittenhouse

- **"True North"** – Bill George

- **"Leading Without Power – Finding Hope in Serving Community"** – Max DePree

- **"Heart-Centered Leadership: An Invitation to Lead from the Inside Out"** – Susan Steinbrecher & Joel Bennett

- **"A Cross – A Heart & A Flag"** – Peggy Noonan

"The measure of our progress in civilization is the degree to which we bring our economic motivation into harmony with our ethical aspirations."

James Cash Penney

CHAPTER FIVE

"The harder the conflict, the more glorious the triumph. What we obtain too cheaply, we esteem too lightly; 'tis dearness only that gives everything its value. I love the man who can smile in trouble, who can gather strength from distress and grow brave by reflection. 'Tis the business of little minds to shrink; but he whose heart is firm, and whose conscience approves his conduct, will pursue his principles unto death."

Thomas Paine

COMMITMENT

Key Principle this Week: Commitment

"Until one is committed, there is hesitancy, the chance to draw back, always ineffectiveness. Concerning all acts of initiative (and creation), there is one elementary truth – ignorance of which kills countless ideas and splendid plans: That the moment one definitely commits oneself, then Providence moves, too. All sorts of things occur to help one that never otherwise would have occurred. A whole stream of events issues from decision, raising in one's favor all manner of unforeseen incidents and meetings and material assistance, which no man could have dreamed would have come his way.
Whatever you can do, or dream you can, begin it.
Boldness has genius, power and magic in it. Begin it now!"

Johann Goethe

Commitment: *a state of being emotionally or intellectually bound to a course of action or person; a pledge; maintaining our promises; keeping our word, regardless of the payback.*

Commitment can be a very powerful word. And the words that are used to define it are also strong words – bound, maintaining and keeping. They imply staying with things. There is not a lot of wiggle room in these words.

To some, a commitment is a promise that people can count on. To others, it's either a loose expression of what they'd like to see happen, or a statement that lacks real meaning. These kinds of statements might be made when a commitment is being sought, but if something better comes along, the deal is off. Too often our commitments can be shallow, without real intent to follow through. We say yes quickly, and then it hits us later what that might mean.

God promised he would love us and then demonstrated his commitment by sending a Messiah into the world whose whole life was about living for that love. And then the ultimate expression of commitment, he died for his friends. When thinking about commitment, ask yourself who or what is at the center of your life?

I Choose Commitment...

I do not want to live a wishy-washy life.
I want to stand for what I say.
I pray this week for the renewal of my most important
commitment to you, Lord.
Let me take a rejuvenated heart into all of my other
commitments such that people can really count on me.
Because I choose to be committed.

COMMITMENT

DELIVER ON YOUR PROMISES

"Be the change you are trying to create."
Mohandas K. Gandhi

The old adage that says "actions speak louder than words" is true and this little man understood it clearly. He helped make huge changes in India by delivering on his convictions and words. These kinds of commitments are made in the heart - in the inner-most depths of our being.

Many successful leaders have built their reputations, at least in part, by sticking with their commitments and allowing those around them to see that they can be counted on. This is how trust is built. Often, the grass looks green on the other side, but letting "your yes be yes" is one of the things the Bible advocates. Stick with your promises and deliver on your commitments…be that change…in spite of your fears !

Today's Journal

To what are you really committed? And why?

_____

_____

_____

_____

_____

_____

_____

_____

_____

_____

_____

_____

_____

_____

_____

_____

_____

_____

_____

Action Step – What one thing will you do today about these thoughts?

_____

_____

_____

_____

_____

COMMITMENT

Nurture Covenant Relationships

"The primary way to prepare for the unknown is to attend to the quality of our relationships,
to how well we know and trust one another."

Meg Wheatley

Commitments generally occur in relationship with others. And the quality of those relationships, how deeply you connect, how real you are, indicates whether it goes beyond being just another of many acquaintances.

In the marketplace, leaders use covenant relationships with others like key staff, special customers or suppliers to build their business. When people know they can count on you, anything is possible. Loyalty increases and trust grows. If you're fulfilling the needs of others, business will grow as well.

And, it's just as true at home in your marriage and family relationships. Relationships - not money – is really what makes the world go 'round.

Today's Journal

To whom are you really committed?

_____

_____

_____

_____

_____

_____

_____

_____

_____

_____

_____

_____

_____

_____

_____

_____

_____

_____

_____

_____

Action Step – What one thing will you do today about these thoughts?

_____

_____

_____

_____

_____

COMMITMENT

BE STEADFAST

> _"Commitment through adversity builds character, perspective_
> _and vision into the life of a leader."_
> **Sid Buzzell**

When adversity strikes or when problems arise, this is the time to examine what "commitment" really means to you. Sometimes our promises slip away when other demands come along, when we change our minds or when better ideas present themselves. Oft times we say we're simply being flexible.

But leaders who keep their word build trust. Maintaining an attitude of commitment requires constant vigilance, both on the front end in what you say, and later in fulfilling those promises or creating new agreements. An attitude of humble determination, with heavy doses of patience, will help you be steadfast...and it builds character.

Today's Journal

What gets in your way of being fully committed?

_____

_____

_____

_____

_____

_____

_____

_____

_____

_____

_____

_____

_____

_____

_____

_____

_____

_____

_____

_____

_____

Action Step – What one thing will you do today about these thoughts?

_____

_____

_____

_____

_____

COMMITMENT

TAKE A STAND

> *"Then Solomon stood before the altar of the Lord in front of the whole assembly*
> *of Israel, spread out his hands toward heaven and said; "O Lord, God of Israel,*
> *there is no God like you in heaven above or on earth below – you who keep your*
> *covenant of love with your servants who continue wholeheartedly in your way.*
> *Your have kept your promise to your servant David my father;*
> *with your mouth you have promised and with your*
> *hand you have fulfilled it."*
>
> ### 1 Kings 8: 22-24

Solomon's public declaration was a powerful statement to a large body of people. With his hands lifted to heaven, there was probably no misunderstanding as to where he stood. His clear affirmation of faith was a guiding light to Israel.

When leaders express their convictions they're taking a stand. They're making verbal commitments, and in a sense, asking others to hold them to their promises. It's one thing to make a commitment to yourself to do something, but when others know, you've increased the stakes. For example, when you publicly declare that unethical behavior will not be tolerated, you're asking everyone in the organization to hold each other accountable for proper conduct. The involvement of others simply increases your commitment.

Today's Journal

When was the last time you took a stand and made a public declaration?

_____

_____

_____

_____

_____

_____

_____

_____

_____

_____

_____

_____

_____

_____

_____

_____

_____

_____

_____

_____

_____

Action Step – What one thing will you do today about these thoughts?

_____

_____

_____

_____

_____

COMMITMENT

REALIZE ACTIONS SPEAK LOUDEST

> _"What you do speaks so loud that I cannot hear what you say."_
> **Ralph Waldo Emerson**

Intentions can be good but actions tell the extent of our commitments. One might assume Emerson is directing his thought here to the person whose actions don't line-up with his words and thus he really isn't heard. Imagine if that's you.

In the organizational realm, commitments come in many sizes and varieties, like promises to deliver a report by a certain date or the promise of a raise. At the most basic level, think of how you view being on time. Do you make an effort to always be there when you said you would, or doesn't it matter that much? It may seem trite, but working diligently to be on time is probably indicative of how you hold other commitments.

Good leaders model commitment, they let their actions speak before they ask others to follow. Interestingly, your words might be heard this way !

Today's Journal

Describe a situation when people really counted on you and you delivered? What was that like?

_____

_____

_____

_____

_____

_____

_____

_____

_____

_____

_____

_____

_____

_____

_____

_____

_____

_____

Action Step – What one thing will you do today about these thoughts?

_____

_____

_____

_____

COMMITMENT

Take a moment to look back over your notes this week. Do your entries still resonate with you? Would you add anything?

And, how did you do on the actions steps you gave yourself? Be tough on yourself. If you didn't move on something, ask yourself why. And when you understand that "why", go just a little deeper and ask yourself again, why you want that outcome.

Comment here with additional thoughts and with whatever else you need to do about your notes and actions.

_____
_____
_____
_____
_____

Here are a few references on "commitment" that might be helpful.

- **"Theodore Rex"** – Edmund Morris

- **"Gandhi – The Story of My Experiments with Truth"** – Mohandas K. Gandhi

- **"We Were Soldiers Once and Young"** – Harold G. Moore

- **"Long Walk to Freedom"** – Nelson Mandela

- **"Shackleton's Way – Leadership Lessons from the Great Antarctic Explorer"** – Margot Morrell & Stephanie Capparell

- **"When Character Was King – A Story of Ronald Reagan"** – Peggy Noonan

"The probability that we may fail in the struggle ought not to deter us from the support of a cause we believe to be just."

Abraham Lincoln

CHAPTER SIX

*"There is very little difference in people, but that little difference
makes a big difference.
The little difference is attitude. The big difference is
whether it is positive or negative."*

Clement Stone

ATTITUDE

Key Principle this Week: Attitude

"We who have lived in concentration camps can remember the men who walked through the huts comforting others, giving away their last piece of bread. They may have been few in number, but they offer sufficient proof that everything can be taken from man but one thing: the last of the human freedoms – to choose one's attitude in any given set of circumstances – to choose one's own way."

Viktor Frankl

Attitude: *an overall outlook on life; a mind-set or way of thinking that affects everything that you do; your demeanor or mood.*

As we delve into attitude this week, we'll look at a variety of important dimensions, including courage, humility, enthusiasm, optimism and joy. And you could easily add to this list confidence, passion, patience and humor. Think about an attitude of gratitude – what does it take to come from that perspective? On the other hand, think what about the nerve it takes to ask for help. Or the fear of failing that arises in you when faced with a serious challenge. These emotions can become very real…and very large.

While it's more common to promote a positive attitude, negative aspects can pop-up quite easily - like arrogance, selfishness, complaining, comparing and judging others. During World War II, General Douglas MacArthur turned a negative into a positive when he said, "we're not retreating – we're advancing in a different direction." [1]

A positive attitude is a huge asset for leaders and often helps them to take courageous, but calculated risks. If we just take a few minutes, especially first thing each morning, to reflect through prayer and meditation, we can discover a positive perspective.

I CHOOSE A POSITIVE ATTITUDE...

I can be afraid, or I can take a reasonable risk.
I can think only about myself, or I can offer a helping hand.
I refuse to be cynical.
Instead, I will look for the gift in what you say.
I will smile and say "thank you" to those who I encounter,
and I will say I'm sorry when I screw-up.
Today, I will be a better, stronger, more balanced person.
And thus, today, I choose a positive attitude !

ATTITUDE

HAVE THE COURAGE OF YOUR CONVICTIONS

> _"It is not the critic who counts; not the man who points out how the
> strong man stumbles, or where the doer of deeds could have done better.
> The credit belongs to the man who is actually in the arena, whose face is
> marred by dust and sweat and blood; who strives valiantly; who errs, and
> comes up short again and again, because there is no effort without error
> and shortcoming; who knows the great enthusiasms, the great devotions;
> who spends himself in a worthy cause; who at the best knows in the end the
> triumph of high achievement, and who at the worst, if he fails, at least fails
> while daring greatly, so that his place shall never be with
> those cold and timid souls
> who know neither victory nor defeat."_
>
> **_Theodore Roosevelt_**

President Roosevelt really laid down the gauntlet with this declaration.
Too often, it's the cynics who make the most noise in searching for
even the smallest fault. But a leader with conviction can stand against
these negatives because he knows he will learn and grow, one way or
the other.

Real maturity comes more from your mistakes than your successes.
And your courage to lead others is greatly enhanced by understanding
your values and beliefs. Convictions are about deep commitments to
what you stand for. Courage is not wavering from these convictions!

Today's Journal

What does courage mean to you?

_____

_____

_____

_____

_____

_____

_____

_____

_____

_____

_____

_____

_____

_____

_____

_____

_____

_____

Action Step – What one thing will you do today about these thoughts?

_____

_____

_____

_____

_____

ATTITUDE

NOT KNOWING PRODUCES HUMILITY

>_"For everyone who exalts himself will be humbled,_
>_and he who humbles himself will be exalted."_
>### **Luke 18:14**

This biblical story about the Pharisee and the tax collector points toward being other-centered versus self-centered. It highlights a serving attitude rather than puffing-up and bragging.

Leaders are often looked to for the answer. And many times you'll have an idea or a suggestion, but not always. Saying "I don't know" requires a willingness to be vulnerable…maybe even wrong. It calls for the ability to listen to others and to not have to be right about everything. The character trait of humility can be tied to a more modest, curious nature about the thoughts of others. The opposite is an attitude of arrogance and superiority. Since God gave us free will, you choose !

Today's Journal

Describe a situation when you said "I don't know."

_____

_____

_____

_____

_____

_____

_____

_____

_____

_____

_____

_____

_____

_____

_____

_____

_____

_____

_____

Action Step – What one thing will you do today about these thoughts?

_____

_____

_____

_____

_____

ATTITUDE

SEEING THE POSSIBLE

> *"We can't always control the invasion of change, but we can control our responses. The only sure fact we know about change is that it will continue. Only when our attitude toward change becomes positive and we learn to view change as an opportunity, will we begin to unleash our full potential."*
>
> ### Keith Harrell

Change is inevitable. We can't stop it and we generally don't like it. And the only person that likes change is a baby in a wet diaper.

When change is upon us, seeing the possible is a huge asset. Most successful leaders have learned the trait of optimism and they know that a confident, forward-looking attitude speaks to the extent of their commitment. Stepping out with passion attracts others to your cause and can turn change into opportunity.

Today's Journal

How does seeing "the glass as half full or half empty" affect your decisions?

_____

_____

_____

_____

_____

_____

_____

_____

_____

_____

_____

_____

_____

_____

_____

_____

_____

_____

_____

Action Step – What one thing will you do today about these thoughts?

_____

_____

_____

_____

_____

ATTITUDE

Be Enthusiastic

"You cannot kindle a fire in any other heart until it is burning in your own."
Unknown

Enthusiasm, derived from the Greek for spirit, is one of the things that inspires others to action, even while it pushes fear and worry away. Enthusiasm is contagious, but you can't instill it in others unless you've got it yourself.

Greeting people with "I'm feeling great today" rather than just "fine" or "OK" can set the tone for your conversations.   What if you ended a conversation with "God bless your day" versus just "talk to you later." Think about how a smile communicates an attitude that can be infectious.   George Bernard Shaw once said, "a candle loses nothing by lighting another." [2]

And a good belly laugh can really feel great too.   People just naturally want to be around others who are upbeat. Enthusiasm is an attitude that we can choose. Why wouldn't you?

Today's Journal

Describe the attitude of someone who affects you in a positive way.

_____

_____

_____

_____

_____

_____

_____

_____

_____

_____

_____

_____

_____

_____

_____

_____

_____

Action Step – What one thing will you do today about these thoughts?

_____

_____

_____

_____

_____

ATTITUDE

START YOUR DAY RIGHT

*"Listening to God each morning fills you with expectancy
and favor for a better day,
and those days add up to a better life."*

Joyce Meyer

In her book, <u>Start Your Day Right</u>, Joyce Meyer recommends that from the moment your eyes open, begin to set your heart on good things. She provides a consistent message to begin each day in reflection, meditation or prayer…and then to listen for a prompting.

This kind of a beginning allows you to experience the joy of being alive. As you get into the day, regardless of the challenges or decisions you face, that joy can set the tone and influence your attitude throughout the day.   Great leaders infect those around them.

So, when you greet the dawn with a positive attitude, expect good things at sunset.

<u>*Today's Journal*</u>

What most often brings you joy?

_____

_____

_____

_____

_____

_____

_____

_____

_____

_____

_____

_____

_____

_____

_____

_____

_____

<u>*Action Step – What one thing will you do today about these thoughts?*</u>

_____

_____

_____

_____

_____

ATTITUDE

Take a moment to look back over your notes this week. Do your entries still resonate with you? Would you add anything?

And, how did you do on the actions steps you outlined? Be tough on yourself. If you didn't move on something, ask yourself why. And when you understand that "why", go just a little deeper and ask yourself again, why you want that outcome.

Comment here with additional thoughts and with whatever else you need to do about your notes and actions.

_____

_____

_____

_____

_____

_____

Here are a few references on "attitude" that might be helpful.

- **"Attitude is Everything: A Tune-up to Enhance your Life"** - Keith D. Harrell

- **"Enthusiasm Makes the Difference"** – Norman Vincent Peale

- **"Awaken the Giant Within"** – Anthony Robbins

- **"The Magic of Thinking Big"** – David J. Schwartz

- **"Start Your Day Right"** – Joyce Meyer

"Nothing can dim the light which shines from within."

Maya Angelou

PART III
JOURNALING ON SKILLS

This realm or domain covers both strategic and tactical skills that we use out in the world. These are principles with a pronounced action-orientation that move things and people forward toward producing desired results. While character is the bedrock of leadership, we must be prepared to take skillful action.

VISION – COMMUNICATING
LEARNING – EXECUTING

CHAPTER SEVEN

"Leaders are visionaries with a poorly developed sense of fear and no concept of the odds against them."

Robert Jarvik

VISION

Key Principle this Week: Vision

"You see things and say, 'why?'
But I dream things that never were and say 'why not?'"

George Bernard Shaw

Vision: *a description of where you want to be in the future, perhaps a 5-10 year timeframe; a picture of what it will look and feel like when you are achieving your dream.*

Casting a vision is an essential and extremely valuable leadership principle. In his book <u>Visionary Leadership</u>, Burt Nanus defines vision as "a realistic, credible, attractive future for your organization. It is the indispensable tool without which leadership is doomed to failure." [1]

Leaders see what others don't. They look for what is coming next. And while visioning is a skill that helps us paint vivid pictures, for it to be significant, it requires having an executable strategy that evolves in relationship with others.

Creating a powerful vision by yourself has less meaning than doing it with others. For a vision to be fully realized, leaders must build trust with those around them. They've got to invest the time to engage others deeply. It's one way that leaders develop followers - just as the Man from Galilee did. And his most famous prayer was interpreted by John Ortberg when he saw God's vision as; "Make it down here like it is up there." [2]

I Choose to be Visionary

I am thankful for the opportunity to

envision a better world.

I want to have a direction…

I want to know where I'm going.

But I also want to know how I'm going to get there.

And who be will with me?

I pray for guidance this week in touching those around me.

For even though I know things will evolve,

I choose to have a vision !

VISION

ENVISION FUTURES OF HOPE

> *"So we fix our eyes not on what is seen, but on what is unseen.*
> *For what is seen is temporary, but what is unseen is eternal."*
>
> ### 2 Corinthians 4:18

In his letter to the Corinthians, Paul was pointing toward a compelling vision of eternity. He knew that we could not fully comprehend what lay ahead, so he asked us to simply have faith and trust.

Visionary leaders can sense what some around them often miss. They're always looking ahead for a foretaste of what's needed – what's lacking in society. Leaders must paint pictures of brighter futures where life is better and people are helped in a multitude of ways. Many leaders with these tendencies are voracious readers. They tend to be up on the news, but also are well read in history and philosophy. They look for emerging trends and try to link the major threads of our culture into a picture of what might be coming.

Once you've got a vivid image it should be written out, clarified and spoken repeatedly. Casting a vision for organizations, as Stephen Covey so aptly says, is about "having the end in mind." [3] Because visionaries who are effective are not dreamers. They create strategies and plans. They move toward their vision - one step at a time.

Today's Journal

As you envision the next ten years, how does an eternal perspective play in your thinking?

_____

_____

_____

_____

_____

_____

_____

_____

_____

_____

_____

_____

_____

_____

_____

_____

_____

_____

Action Step – What one thing will you do today about these thoughts?

_____

_____

_____

_____

_____

VISION

> *"The challenge of statesmanship is to have the vision to*
> *dream of a better, safer world,*
> *and the courage, persistence and patience to turn that dream into reality."*
>
> **Ronald Reagan**

More than anything else, Ronald Reagan was driven by a thirst for freedom. He knew that democracy brought hope and the creative spark to people. That vision for a better world was developed early in his childhood primarily from the faith of his mother.

What does it mean to have courage for your convictions? While Webster refers to bravery in facing danger, another way of looking at courage is as a reflection of the heart, of something deep within. Courage is not rooted in reason, but rather comes from a divine purpose to make things right. As President, Reagan stepped out against the "evil empire" in the Soviet Union in spite of criticism from the cultural elite. The result changed the world.

But what of patience? Change, particularly significant change, takes time. Usually a lot more than we initially expect. Patience is that elusive trait that when blended with commitment to an important cause will usually produce results. Just keep in mind that God's got a plan and a timetable for everything and one of our jobs is to understand it !

Today's Journal

When you are realizing your vision, how will your life be different?

_____

_____

_____

_____

_____

_____

_____

_____

_____

_____

_____

_____

_____

_____

_____

_____

_____

_____

_____

Action Step – What one thing will you do today about these thoughts?

_____

_____

_____

_____

_____

VISION

ACT BOLDLY ON YOUR VISION

> _"Vision without action is just a dream. Action without vision is just passing time. Vision with action can change the world."_
>
> **Unknown**

Dreams can be good. And taking action is usually better than sitting on your hands. But doing something that moves your vision forward makes all the difference.

Taking bold action is one of those virtues that sets leaders apart. The best action is that which follows a plan. Empowering leaders paint inspiring big pictures of futures worth striving for. They describe a potential worth passing on to future generations. If your vision is worthy of both your effort and of those you call around you, then it's good enough to lay out a roadmap. How will you get there? What will it take? Who needs to join your movement to make it both successful and significant?

And then once you have the plan, remember that you have to work it. Plans always change and evolve. But if you don't act on the strategies and tactics that you've laid out, then what's the use - it's just a dream !

Today's Journal

What holds you back from taking action?

_____

_____

_____

_____

_____

_____

_____

_____

_____

_____

_____

_____

_____

_____

_____

_____

_____

_____

_____

Action Step – What one thing will you do today about these thoughts?

_____

_____

_____

_____

_____

VISION

SET AN EXAMPLE

"Be the change you want to see in the world."
Mohandas Gandhi

He was a little man tackling big challenges. He didn't have an army or even a tangible organization behind him. He simply knew in his heart what was needed and what was right and he committed himself to doing something about it.

Similarly, organizational leaders must identify the needs of society and take action that respond to those needs. But words on paper won't do it. You have to set the example and be the change yourself. Gandhi's march to the sea for salt is a wonderful story that makes this point. He needed to rally the Indian people behind independence in a non-violent way. So, he simply set out to march to the Indian Ocean to show the Brits he meant business, and before long thousands were right there with him. By being the change, he altered the British Empire forever !

Today's Journal

What is the change you want to see in the world?

_____

_____

_____

_____

_____

_____

_____

_____

_____

_____

_____

_____

_____

_____

_____

_____

_____

_____

Action Step – What one thing will you do today about these thoughts?

_____

_____

_____

_____

VISION

ENGAGE OTHERS

"Come, follow me, and I will make you fishers of men."
Matthew 4:19

The Man from Galilee called his followers to a larger purpose. He recognized that his task would require many other leaders to take up his yoke after he was called home.

Effective leaders must attract others to their cause rather than trying to carry the ball by themselves. For leaders to be successful, they must create trust between and among their followers. They must really spend the time to understand them at the heart level. They must get below the surface of "what's new" to truly understand what's needed. To paraphrase a famous line, "people don't care how much you know, until they know how much you care." [4] At this level, trust can be built over time. And when it is, visions of the future become believable.

Jim Collins, in his book <u>Good to Great</u>, describes the process as "getting the right people on the bus." [5] And in some cases "getting the wrong people off the bus." Inherent in creating a legacy is leaving behind other leaders who will carry the torch. In the final analysis, it's all about people. And the movement that started near Galilee is still evolving!

Today's Journal

What do you do to connect at the heart level with those closest to you?

_____

_____

_____

_____

_____

_____

_____

_____

_____

_____

_____

_____

_____

_____

_____

_____

_____

_____

Action Step – What one thing will you do today about these thoughts?

_____

_____

_____

_____

_____

VISION

Take a moment to look back over your notes this week. Do your entries still resonate with you? Would you add anything?

And, how did you do on the actions steps you gave yourself? Be tough on yourself. If you didn't move on something, ask yourself why. And when you understand that "why", go just a little deeper and ask yourself again, why you want that outcome.

Comment here with additional thoughts and with whatever else you need to do about your notes and actions.

_____

_____

_____

_____

_____

Here are a few references on "vision" that might be helpful.

- **"When Character Was King – A Story of Ronald Reagan"** – Peggy Noonan

- **"Visionary Leadership"** – Burt Nanus

- **"Repacking Your Bags for the Rest of Your Life"** – Richard Leider

- **"From Success to Significance"** – Lloyd Reeb

- **"Gandhi – An Autobiography – The Story of My Experiments with Truth"** – Mohandas K. Gandhi

- **"Long Walk to Freedom"** – Nelson Mandela

"In every block of marble I see a statue; see it as plainly as though it stood before me, shaped and perfect in attitude and action. I have only to hew away the rough walls which imprison the lovely apparition to reveal it to other eyes, as mine already see it."

Michelangelo

CHAPTER EIGHT

*"Effective leaders put words to the formless longings
and deeply felt needs of others."*
Warren Bennis

COMMUNICATING

Key Principle this Week: Communicating

"Leadership is about creating day by day the domain in which we and those around us continually deepen our understanding of reality and are able to participate in shaping the future. This, then, is the deeper territory of leadership, collectively listening to what is wanting to emerge in the world, and then having the courage to do what is required."

Joseph Jaworski

<u>Communicating</u>: *the art and process of creating understanding; expressing oneself in such a way that one is clearly understood.*

Communicating is probably one of the most difficult leadership skills, and at the same time, one of the most critical. Effective leaders must be able to get their message across. Whether it's an idea or a request, you've got to be clear. But communicating can be complex because people are complex. That's probably why so many books have been written and so many courses are offered on the subject. But beyond all of the good techniques, think of communications as a means of touching another's soul rather than an end in itself.

The purpose of communicating should be creating a shared perspective between and among people. Communication has been called "the beginning of understanding" and is a primary means of building solid relationships. Powerful communication is not about being right or winning the conversation, but really about learning. That's why one aspect of inside-first leadership is more about asking good questions than about having the right answer. It's a two-way process.

Communicating has both an active side and a passive side. The active side is about expressing oneself and includes many proven techniques, like feedback, rapport-building, and knowing your audience. Effective leaders often use stories and metaphor to simplify their core message. They speak from the heart rather than a script. In this respect, scripture reminds us that "out of the overflow of the heart the mouth speaks." And lastly, remember that your actions are a significant form of your communication.

The more passive side is the willingness of a quiet, still heart that yearns to understand. Listening is the key approach here, but that is sometimes a lost art in today's technology-driven culture. Ever notice how we aren't really listening, but rather formulating our response? Leaders have an unusual responsibility to listen well, not only for information, but for feelings as well.

Then there's writing or journaling as a powerful way to express one's thoughts. Writing it down requires discipline, thoughtfulness and time. And there are many media available; beyond words are video, photography and art. Then there is body language and eye contact.

So, it's probably obvious that the dimensions of communication are vast and often complex, and yet critical for effective, ethical leadership.

I Choose to Communicate fully...

I want to understand you - I want to know you.
I want to be clear with you.
For understanding you at a deep level allows me to know your heart.
And if I know your heart, I know you.

That's why I choose to communicate fully !

COMMUNICATING

LISTEN FIRST

> *"God gave two ears and just one mouth.*
> *So we ought to listen at least twice as much as we talk."*
>
> **Lawrence Richards**

When the subject of communications comes up, many people immediately think of expressing themselves, of making their point. Richards reminds us here that it is about more than speaking!

Maybe you think that listening is that part of communications reserved for the other guy. You feel you've got to be clear and compelling, maybe even profound or visionary in what you say. But if a fundamental purpose of communications is to increase understanding among the parties, then Covey has it right with "seek first to understand." [1]

And if listening is based on the notion that we don't know everything, then asking a question first makes a connection and establishes interest. If you just listen and avoid interrupting, after a few minutes, you almost earn the right to then be heard. By being respectful and abstaining from corrections, a more robust dialogue can evolve. Making others wrong just isn't very effective, while working on our listening skills can be a significant part of improving.

Today's Journal

What barriers do you experience in being a more effective listener?

_____

_____

_____

_____

_____

_____

_____

_____

_____

_____

_____

_____

_____

_____

_____

_____

_____

Action Step – What one thing will you do today about these thoughts?

_____

_____

_____

_____

_____

COMMUNICATING

BE COMFORTABLE NOT KNOWING

"Seek first to understand – then to be understood."
Stephen Covey

One way to appreciate the complexity of communications is from the perspective of "not knowing." Realizing that you don't have to have all the answers is central to effective communications, and by embracing this approach, understanding becomes easier. When you listen to the other guy, really trying to comprehend, he's then more likely to listen to you.

Getting outside of yourself, beyond your own self-righteousness, is the key. But this is easier said than done. Effective leaders know that communicating is not about having to win the conversation. It's really about understanding. In the give-and-take of real dialogue, when we're beyond trying to be right, we can really learn something.

An unknown sage once said; "Language is how we give shape to the spirit moving through us." And it's in these kinds of conversations that healthy relationships are built.

Today's Journal

When you think you have to have the answer, what is motivating you?

_____

_____

_____

_____

_____

_____

_____

_____

_____

_____

_____

_____

_____

_____

_____

_____

_____

_____

Action Step – What one thing will you do today about these thoughts?

_____

_____

_____

_____

_____

COMMUNICATING

KNOW THAT CHARACTER SHAPES OUR WORDS

> _"What you do speaks so loudly that I cannot hear what you say."_
> **Ralph Waldo Emerson**

Communicating is more character-based than skill-based. Surely we must draw upon all the various techniques available, but our words are mostly informed by our character. And character shows up in our actions.

Character is built on values, those beliefs and virtues that we treasure. And while there is a range of values we each hold dear, authentic leaders tend to value traits like authenticity and compassion over recognition and wealth. When our character is based on good values, we tend to listen more and tame the tongue to speak from the heart.

Like a virtuous cycle, our actions then signal our character. The well-known expression – our actions speak louder than our words – embellishes what Emerson was saying. Effective communication occurs, and people really get what we are saying, when they see what we do. Integrity is the character-based trait that results when our actions are consistent with our words.

Today's Journal

How does your character influence you as a communicator?

_____

_____

_____

_____

_____

_____

_____

_____

_____

_____

_____

_____

_____

_____

_____

_____

_____

_____

_____

_____

Action Step – What one thing will you do today about these thoughts?

_____

_____

_____

_____

_____

COMMUNICATING

BUILD RELATIONSHIPS

> *"Communication is the foundation for all successful relationships,*
> *and rapport is the foundation of all successful communication."*
> **Leslie Sholl Jaffe**

Communication occurs between and among people…in relationships. And the nature of the relationship, often times, determines the nature of the communications. Strong leaders tend to know their audience - they establish rapport - they build relationships.

Relationships can take many diverse shapes, like parent to child; friend to friend; or leader to follower. But regardless of the form, you are fundamentally either a giver or a taker in those relationships. The giver is interested in helping others - the taker is more interested in helping himself. Nelson Mandela was a giver who felt he was called to serve, teaching that relationships, and countries, tend to grow when you are other-centered versus self-centered.

Today's Journal

In a valued relationship, ask what is the most important thing we can talk about today? What is that topic?

_____

_____

_____

_____

_____

_____

_____

_____

_____

_____

_____

_____

_____

_____

_____

_____

_____

_____

_____

_____

Action Step – What one thing will you do today about these thoughts?

_____

_____

_____

_____

_____

COMMUNICATING

"The power of questions is rooted in an attitude of curiosity,
of really wanting to know."

Anonymous

Communicating at its most fundamental level is a two-way process of understanding. All of us would like to "be" clear in our communications, but "becoming" clear probably more accurately describes the progression. And as such, communicating generally involves a lot of back-and-forth, what the experts call "feedback."

In the spoken medium, feedback clarifies through statements like; "So, I understand you to mean…" Or a thoughtful question can help further draw out what is meant. One approach is to ask for an example that portrays the situation. Ask a lot of why questions - keep drilling down to try to understand. Whatever the form, feedback recognizes that meaning resides with the listener, not the speaker.

In your own self-reflection, ask "why do I want something?" And once you've got that answer, ask again, "so why do I want *that*?" And so on until you become clear at a very root level.

Today's Journal

Describe a current situation where communicating is severely challenged. What is going on in the relationship? What questions could you ask to help move things along?

_____

_____

_____

_____

_____

_____

_____

_____

_____

_____

_____

_____

_____

_____

_____

_____

_____

_____

Action Step – What one thing will you do today about these thoughts?

_____

_____

_____

_____

COMMUNICATING

Take a moment to look back over your notes this week. Do your entries still resonate with you? Would you add anything?

And, how did you do on the actions steps you outlined? Be tough on yourself. If you didn't move on something, ask yourself why. And when you understand that "why", go just a little deeper and ask yourself again, why you want that outcome.

Comment here with additional thoughts and with whatever else you need to do about your notes and actions.

_____

_____

_____

_____

_____

Here are a few references on "communicating" that might be helpful.

- **"Fierce Conversations: Achieving Success at Work & in Life – One Conversation at a Time"** – Susan Scott

- **"Crucial Conversations"** – Kerry Patterson

- **"Getting to Yes – Negotiating Agreement Without Giving In"** – Roger Fisher & William Ury

- **"Listening Leaders: The Ten Golden Rules to Listen, Lead & Succeed"** Lyman Steil & Richard Bommelje

- **"A Hidden Wholeness: The Journey Toward an Undivided Life"** Parker Palmer

"For out of the overflow of his heart, his mouth speaks."

Luke 6:45

CHAPTER NINE

*"Wisdom has to do with our relationship to the whole, to the cosmos, to nature,
to both the feminine and the masculine powers of nature.
Wisdom is finding the balance between head and heart."*

Matthew Fox

LEARNING

KEY PRINCIPLE THIS WEEK: LEARNING

"The behavior we call leadership is, before it is anything else, an initiative from within oneself. Leadership has self-direction as its essence, for to communicate to anyone else what ought to be done, a leader must first have communicated it, however loosely, to himself or herself. So the crucial learning process for a leader is learning what he or she wants to see happen."

Peter Vaill

Learning: *an orientation toward acquiring knowledge and gaining wisdom; more about an attitude of growing and less about the rigors of institutional education; tied more to questions than answers.*

Frederic Hudson, the sage executive coach said, "If you're not growing, you're dying." [1] By growing he meant learning, expanding your perspective, trying something new. With technology, it has become easier to both stay connected and to uncover knowledge. This makes learning more readily available. But learning what? All wisdom scripture asks that we build our learning on doing what is good and right and helpful. Everything we need to know about behavior, ethics, and every other key leadership issue is contained somewhere in those scriptures.

But how does one turn learning into wisdom? Simply stated, it most often comes with experience and maturity. Learning the lessons of life can be difficult, particularly in our early years. But over time a more patient, more spiritual approach seems to bring us answers more readily. Understanding can often be gained in interaction with others, particularly in small groups, where dialogue allows the lessons we've all learned to come out in a supportive, loving fashion. Wisdom is earned, not acquired.

Some leaders, however, view knowledge as all-powerful. Market knowledge; technological know-how; intellectual capital. The reality is that knowledge is good, but it's not the primary thing that makes the world go 'round. Effective leaders know that it's more about people and how we relate to one another.

Too often, learning is thought of as something only done in school. But the process of continuous maturation that occurs all throughout life is best fueled by an attitude of "not knowing", of longing to understand and the joy of freely asking the "why" and "how" questions. The title of Peter Vaill's book quoted above expresses what we all might strive for - <u>Learning as a Way of Being</u>.

I Choose to Learn

I am thankful for my curious nature
and for the opportunities that cross my path,
for I know that wisdom really comes from above.
And so I pray that I would keep my eyes and ears open
to all the splendor around me,
because I choose to keep learning.

LEARNING

CONTINUOUSLY SHARPEN YOUR PERSPECTIVES

> _"Truth is an eternal conversation about things that matter,_
> _conducted with passion and discipline."_
> **Parker Palmer**

Palmer reminds us here that learning is a process. It's a journey that goes on for your entire life. Imagine the time wasted in mundane conversations of restaurants and cars and other meaningless chit chat.

What are conversations that matter? They tend to be about the deeper questions of life, about purpose, about relationships with people you trust, about matters of the spirit. And even though the conventional wisdom is to avoid politics at dinners, aren't these questions really important? By delving into these issues with a passionate, but open heart, we learn. We learn that understanding the other guy's point-of-view really helps us sharpen our own perspective.

Today's Journal

What are you really passionate about learning?

_____

_____

_____

_____

_____

_____

_____

_____

_____

_____

_____

_____

_____

_____

_____

_____

_____

_____

_____

_____

Action Step – What one thing will you do today about these thoughts?

_____

_____

_____

_____

_____

LEARNING

LEARN FROM YOUR MISTAKES

> _"A mistake is an event you have not yet used to your advantage."_
> **_Edwin Land_**

Your history holds the lessons you've learned, but too often we're not paying much attention. Instead, history repeats itself.

The first step is to acknowledge your mistakes. Sometimes this shortcoming can be very difficult, but when leaders take the initiative to recognize their error, it takes away much of the "charge" from having to be right. This approach can often clear the way to move into solutions. And, an apology goes a long way to mending fences.

Many effective leaders have mentors because learning from others can provide wonderful insight. Asking for advice from those you respect opens the door to wisdom and experience. Almost every challenge that a leader will face has been experienced by someone before you. Reaching out to those sources of knowledge, like a personal board of trustees, can be very powerful. Using these lessons to your advantage just makes good sense.

Today's Journal

What was the circumstance when you last admitted you made a mistake?

_____

_____

_____

_____

_____

_____

_____

_____

_____

_____

_____

_____

_____

_____

_____

_____

_____

_____

Action Step – What one thing will you do today about these thoughts?

_____

_____

_____

_____

_____

LEARNING

TEACH

> *"Give a man a fish, and you'll feed him for a day;*
> *teach a man how to fish, you'll feed him for a lifetime."*
>
> ***Anonymous***

Jesus of Nazareth was definitely a master teacher who also talked about fishing; his plan was about "fishing for men." But teaching is not just for the professionals or prophets; everyone has something to teach and everyone can learn how to fish.

Good leaders are also good teachers - they ask good questions. They take the time to explain their vision and strategy. But teaching is not easy. One of the best ways to learn is to prepare yourself to teach. If you are diligent, you will learn much in the process.

Maturity comes with time, but committing to be a life-long teacher and learner will usually accelerate the process. Continuous learners look at every situation as an opportunity rather than as a barrier. Mature leaders ask - what can I learn from this experience? How can I improve my approach? It's an attitude to take to one's grave.

Today's Journal

What was your most a significant teaching experience over the past several months ?

_____

_____

_____

_____

_____

_____

_____

_____

_____

_____

_____

_____

_____

_____

_____

_____

_____

_____

Action Step – What one thing will you do today about these thoughts?

_____

_____

_____

_____

_____

_____

LEARNING

HAVE AN ATTITUDE OF OPENNESS

"Shall I tell you the secret of the true scholar?
Every man I meet is my master in some point; and in that I learn of him."

Ralph Waldo Emerson

Emerson is reminding us here that none of us have all the answers. We can't be expert in everything. But if we're open to what others know, we can expand our awareness and build our knowledge base.

Successful leaders work hard to create an atmosphere of openness and learning within their organizations. They strive to be amenable to new thinking and new applications. They encourage exploration. They suggest reading and listening to books on tape. They believe in the benefits of being a learning organization.

It's one thing for individual leaders to want to grow, it's quite another for the whole group to be a learning organization. Effective leaders design environments where inquiry is invited and appreciated and where learning is a constant activity. Leaders who cultivate this hunger are likely to be rewarded with engaged followers…and masters of many subjects.

Today's Journal

What inhibits your openness?

_____

_____

_____

_____

_____

_____

_____

_____

_____

_____

_____

_____

_____

_____

_____

_____

_____

_____

_____

_____

Action Step – What one thing will you do today about these thoughts?

_____

_____

_____

_____

_____

Friday

LEARNING

ASK GOOD QUESTIONS

"Ask and it will be given to you; seek and you will find;
knock and the door will be opened to you."
Matthew 7:7

This clear proclamation to "ask" is used by leaders and prayer warriors all the time. Seeking wisdom from above may be one of the great encouragements of all time. But the door probably won't be opened without our effort.

Advanced leaders are able to ask probing questions because they're comfortable with not knowing. This is much easier to say than to do because our culture teaches us about the importance of winning - of being right. The autocratic approach says that bosses ought to have the answers. But in reality, not knowing is often where we are. By seeking to understand others and their perspectives, we add what they know to what we already know. Realizing that it's okay to not know is a huge and important step for leaders. Experiencing the power of the question is even more profound.

The advent of personal and professional coaching is not a wholly new concept, but is another way to draw upon the wisdom of others. A coach can offer leaders alternative perspectives, often by asking just the right question that stimulates the thinking and helps us see situations in new light. Having another set of eyes is usually a good thing.

Today's Journal

Where do you look most often for guidance?

_____

_____

_____

_____

_____

_____

_____

_____

_____

_____

_____

_____

_____

_____

_____

_____

_____

_____

_____

_____

_____

Action Step – What one thing will you do today about these thoughts?

_____

_____

_____

_____

_____

LEARNING

Take a moment to look back over your notes this week. Do your entries still resonate with you? Would you add anything?

And, how did you do on the actions steps you gave yourself? Be tough on yourself. If you didn't move on something, ask yourself why. And when you understand that "why", go just a little deeper and ask yourself again, why you want that outcome.

Comment here with additional thoughts and with whatever else you need to do about your notes and actions.

_____

_____

_____

_____

_____

Here are a few references on "learning" that might be helpful.

1) **"The Courage to Teach – Exploring the Inner Landscape of a Teacher's Life"** – Parker J. Palmer

2) **"Learning as a Way of Being – Strategies for Survival in a World of Permanent White Water"** – Peter B. Vaill

3) **"The Creation of the Future – The Role of the American University"** – Frank H. Rhodes

*"Instruct a wise man and he will be wiser still;
teach a righteous man and he will add to his learning."*

Proverbs 9:9

CHAPTER TEN

"Leadership is about creating day by day the domain in which we and those around us continually deepen our understanding of reality and are able to participate in shaping the future. This, then, is the deeper territory of leadership, collectively listening to what is wanting to emerge in the world, and then having the courage to do what is required."

Joseph Jaworski

EXECUTING

Key Principle this Week: Executing

"Leadership without the discipline of execution is incomplete and ineffective. Without the ability to execute, all other attributes of leadership become hollow."

Larry Bossidy & Ram Charan

<u>Executing</u>: *the discipline of producing the desired results; having a bias for action tied to accountability; a systematic and rigorous process of managing who's going to do what by when.*

Execution makes all the difference because it closes the gap between promises and results. It's all about getting the right things done for the right reasons. That's what leadership is largely about.

As we look at execution this week, we'll touch on the importance of patient planning, praying for guidance, and then initiating, following-up and completing projects. However you want to refer to it - execution, discipline, implementation, action – it's relatively straight-forward stuff. It's the blocking and tackling of leadership. And while it may sound simple, it's definitely not easy.

I Choose to Act

As I plan this week, as I interact and make decisions,
I pray that I will have the courage to execute well.
I know my ideas are usually good, but too often I hold back.
So what if I fail?
If I move forward, at least I will have tried.
I will choose to act!

EXECUTING

PLAN BEFORE DECIDING

> *"Unless you translate big thoughts into concrete steps for action,*
> *they're pointless."*
>
> ### *Larry Bossidy & Ram Charan*

One of the first and most important action steps in execution is making a plan. Laying out those big ideas into a clear and definitive plan creates a roadmap. Once you plan the work, then you can work the plan.

Many leaders in a hurry will follow the "ready – fire – aim" approach just to get things started. While this may produce some immediate activity it doesn't often generate the desired results. Studying the situation, planning thoughtfully and "having the end in mind" [1] , as Stephen Covey advocates, can help leaders understand the factors and forces at play in any challenge. As often as acting, having the patience to plan can be a wonderful demonstration of self-discipline.

Today's Journal

How valuable is making a plan to you?

_____

_____

_____

_____

_____

_____

_____

_____

_____

_____

_____

_____

_____

_____

_____

_____

_____

Action Step – What one thing will you do today about these thoughts?

_____

_____

_____

_____

_____

EXECUTING

REFLECT BEFORE ACTING

> *"Being proactive is more than taking initiative. It is recognizing that we are responsible for our own choices and have freedom to chose based on principles and values rather than on moods or conditions.*
>
> **Stephen R. Covey**

Having the freedom to choose is indeed a blessing of democracy. When we are truly committed to what we stand for, making difficult choices flows from that solid foundation. So, how we go about choosing says a lot about us as leaders.

When making important decisions, most effective leaders will carefully analyze all the available information. They'll apply reasonable logic and try to mesh strategy with reality. The really successful leaders will seek wise counsel from others. It could be their board, trusted colleagues, close friends or family. Many pray and then simply listen. But in all of these approaches, serious reflection plays a role.

After reflection, they decide quickly, according to those values, and then move smartly, communicating the decision widely.

Today's Journal

As you reflect, from whom do you seek counsel?

_____

_____

_____

_____

_____

_____

_____

_____

_____

_____

_____

_____

_____

_____

_____

_____

_____

_____

Action Step – What one thing will you do today about these thoughts?

_____

_____

_____

_____

_____

_____

EXECUTING

TAKE THE FIRST STEP

"In the beginning, God created the heavens and the earth."
Genesis 1:1

God demonstrated one of the critical traits of ultimate leaders by what he created. He took the initiative, he acted rather than reacted, to create heaven and earth. He started something. He took the lead !

Similarly, successful organizational leaders often model this way by taking the first step. They feel a quiet prompting and simply respond by moving ahead. They accept the full responsibility of leadership and avoid just assuming that others will do their part. (Keep in mind that "assume" is one of the most troublesome words in our vocabulary.)

Leaders get specific about dates and deliverables. They make commitments and then keep them. But leaders with a spiritual perspective know the difference between going first and being first. They take the lead, but put God first.

Today's Journal

What most often holds you back from raising your hand and taking the lead?

_____

_____

_____

_____

_____

_____

_____

_____

_____

_____

_____

_____

_____

_____

_____

_____

_____

_____

_____

Action Step – What one thing will you do today about these thoughts?

_____

_____

_____

_____

_____

_____

EXECUTING

*"The way you manage the consequences of people's behavior is one of the most
powerful reward systems in your organization. Your associates take their cues
for what is important, and what is okay
and not okay by what you pay attention to, follow-up on, and measure."*

David P. Hanna

As leaders go about their responsibilities, barriers show-up and boulders
get in the way. Riveting your attention on the desired results can help.
One way to stay focused is by following-up and following through
rigorously.

You may often think that those you lead will completely understand
what you want the first time you ask. You may think that just because
you sent that email that they got it…and have read it. Not always so.
Following-up to ensure there is clarity about the task at hand is one of
the most critical, and productive, leadership activities.

Take 100% responsibility and be relentless about follow-up. And while
you're at it, pause frequently and ask for divine assistance.

Today's Journal

In staying focused on results, what stumbling block do you face most often?

_____

_____

_____

_____

_____

_____

_____

_____

_____

_____

_____

_____

_____

_____

_____

_____

_____

_____

Action Step – What one thing will you do today about these thoughts?

_____

_____

_____

_____

_____

EXECUTING

COMPLETE PROJECTS COMPLETELY

> *"The world is full of very competent people who honestly intend to do things tomorrow, or as soon as they get around to it, but they are seldom a match for people who have developed a balanced sense of urgency, and know how to simply do it now."*
>
> **Unknown**

Completing things ties back to commitment. What is the distinction between intention and commitment? And how committed are you to the things you say you'll do?

Some leaders are very capable of getting things started – launching a new project or kicking off a new service. They are excellent at taking the first step and initiating new work. But oft times, they don't complete the project. They get about two-thirds down the road and then something else grabs their attention. Maybe it's the next idea or even the next crisis. What if you could complete things completely? What would that say about who you are?

Today's Journal

What stands in the way of you really completing things completely?

_____

_____

_____

_____

_____

_____

_____

_____

_____

_____

_____

_____

_____

_____

_____

_____

_____

_____

Action Step – What one thing will you do today about these thoughts?

_____

_____

_____

_____

_____

EXECUTING

Take a moment to look back over your notes this week. Do your entries still resonate with you? Would you add anything?

And, how did you do on the actions steps you gave yourself? Be tough on yourself. If you didn't move on something, ask yourself why. And when you understand that "why", go just a little deeper and ask yourself again, why you want that outcome.

Comment here with additional thoughts and with whatever else you need to do about your notes and actions.

_____

_____

_____

_____

_____

Here are a few references on "executing" that might be helpful.

1) **"Execution: The Discipline of Getting Things Done"** – Larry Bossidy & Ram Charan

2) **"Fierce Conversations: Achieving Success at Work & in Life – One Conversations at a Time"** – Susan Scott

3) **"Leadership"** – Rudi Giuliani

4) **"Getting to Yes"** – Roger Fisher & William Ury

"What might happen is often used as an excuse for not doing what can happen."

Henry Kissenger

PART IV
JOURNALING ON
RELATIONSHIPS

The "relationship" domain recognizes that leaders generally get things done with and through others. Sometimes leadership may seem straight-forward, but things tend to get a little complicated when we involve others. Human nature adds all the complexity we could ever want. But relationships are what make the world go 'round.

SERVING – LOVE
SPIRITUALITY

CHAPTER ELEVEN

"Everybody can be great, because anybody can serve. You don't have to have a college degree to serve. You don't have to know about Plato and Aristotle to serve. You don't have to know Einstein's Theory of Relativity to serve. You only need a heart full of grace and a soul generated by love."

Martin Luther King

SERVING

KEY PRINCIPLE THIS WEEK: SERVING

"Ask not what your country can do for you,
ask what you can do for your country."

John F. Kennedy

Serving: *the act of helping others; a holistic approach to work, promoting a sense of community and shared decision-making; realized when others grow.*

Servant leadership has become more and more common in today's management and organizational development literature. Being of service to others is seen as a worthy and effective strategy.

Serving as a principle parallels the Golden Rule by focusing on others. Robert Greenleaf wrote prolifically about serving in the 1970's and subsequently founded the very successful Center for Servant Leadership in Indianapolis. He said: "It begins with the natural feeling that one wants to serve, then conscious choice brings one to aspire to lead." [1] Greenleaf refers often to the example that the Prince of Peace set by being a servant first.

Caring, compassion, love and genuine interest in others are hallmarks of this philosophy of leadership. It is a giving approach that puts others ahead of ourselves. Stephen Covey said: "A servant leader is one who seeks to draw out, to inspire and develop the best within people from the inside out." [2] Mentoring is a great way of serving where we share ourselves with others.

But understanding servant leadership is not enough. An oft quoted biblical reference says: "Now that you know these things, you will be blessed if you do them."

I CHOOSE TO SERVE...

I am thankful for the blessings of this life,
including the opportunity to serve others.
I pray for a softened my heart this week,
so that I would make myself available to just one person
who needs a helping hand.
I choose to serve simply because it feels right !

Serving

Be Other-Centered

> _"Wisdom relates to trust, humility, teachability, servanthood,_
> _responsiveness and reliance on God;_
> _it is the exact opposite of autonomy and arrogance."_
> ### Sid Buzzell

The underlying premise of the serving principle is being other-centered rather than self-centered. But in a desire-driven, individualistic culture, where arrogance often resides, this concept doesn't get much play. As long as we think that our lives are just about us, about fulfilling our needs only, then we will struggle with serving.

So how does one become other-centered? The best approach comes down to simply recognizing that there is a higher power out there – whatever you choose to call it – and that life is not all about you. George Bernard Shaw admonishes us to be something greater than "a selfish little clod of ailments and grievances complaining that the world will not devote itself to making you happy." [3]

Being a servant leader involves spending some time reflecting on others – their needs and their necessities. Whether it's the marketplace, the classroom or your community, being focused on others, serving others, usually produces meaningful results. Scripture reminds us that "it is more blessed to give than to receive."

Today's Journal

What does being other-centered mean to you?

_____

_____

_____

_____

_____

_____

_____

_____

_____

_____

_____

_____

_____

_____

_____

_____

_____

_____

_____

Action Step – What one thing will you do today about these thoughts?

_____

_____

_____

_____

_____

SERVING

BE AN EXAMPLE

> *"Now that I have washed your feet, you also should wash one another's feet.*
> *I have set you an example that you should do as I have done for you."*
>
> ### John 13: 14-15

In spite of the many advances of our society, we live in a television-dominated culture that focuses on satisfying our personal wants and desires. The prevailing view is that "it's all about me." But, Jesus of Nazareth gave us another model built on serving others. While he set an example with his entire life, washing the disciple's feet was simply one of the most memorable.

How was he able to be other-focused? The answer lies primarily in his security; in who he was, what he stood for and where he was going. Being clear about our purpose, our values and our beliefs can move us toward similar security. And in that security lies the ability to get off our self-serving horse, to understand the needs of others, and simply help someone. Good leaders understand that setting an example for those around them is analogous to the famous expression; "Actions speak louder then words."

Today's Journal

When was the last time you set an example for those around you?
What was that like?

_____

_____

_____

_____

_____

_____

_____

_____

_____

_____

_____

_____

_____

_____

_____

_____

_____

_____

_____

Action Step – What one thing will you do today about these thoughts?

_____

_____

_____

_____

_____

SERVING

CARE ABOUT OTHERS

> _"Do to others as you would have them do to you."_
> **Matthew 7:12**

The root component of the Golden Rule is love; love as manifested in genuine interest in others – having compassion and concern for their needs. For many leaders, love is too squishy, too soft a concept to produce results. But being effective requires a connection, and love is what ties many together.

The Golden Rule is one of those very simple commands that is often so much easier to say than to do. Why is that? Is it because we are primarily concerned about getting ahead? About our own interests? Do we have so much going on in our heads that our hearts are overcome? Are we just too busy to give any thought to the other person?

Stephen Covey's line about "people don't care how much you know, until they know how much you care" [4] says a great deal. Caring is an attitude. Caring is about giving rather than taking. Caring is definitely good – but doing something is even better.

Today's Journal

Describe a situation when you really cared for someone else !

_____
_____
_____
_____
_____
_____
_____
_____
_____
_____
_____
_____
_____
_____
_____
_____
_____
_____

Action Step – What one thing will you do today about these thoughts?

_____
_____
_____
_____
_____

SERVING

MENTOR SOMEONE

> *"Everyone must work to live, but the purpose of life is to serve and to show compassion and the will to help others."*
>
> **Albert Schweitzer**

This great humanitarian doctor devoted his life to helping others. And one of the most meaningful ways to help is to mentor someone.

Mentoring is helping others become successful. It's encouraging them by sharing your gifts and talents. Oft times, mentoring is thought of as something you do just for young people. But the practice of sharing your journey with others can inspire them regardless of their age or station. A close mentor can sometimes become like family where advice and influence is most often sought. And when you treat others like family, compassion is usually present.

Who has been a mentor to you, and how did he or she affect your life?

_____

_____

_____

_____

_____

_____

_____

_____

_____

_____

_____

_____

_____

_____

_____

_____

_____

_____

Action Step – What one thing will you do today about these thoughts?

_____

_____

_____

_____

_____

SERVING

BE A STEWARD

> *"Stewardship begins with the willingness to be accountable and committed to something larger than ourselves – an organization, the community, a high power."*
>
> **Peter Block**

Most good leaders are also good stewards. They develop, and then use, their gifts and talents for a meaningful purpose. Stewards are responsible for realizing a return on the resources entrusted to them, particularly human and financial resources. Although the media would have you believe otherwise, there are many good corporate CEO's who exhibit stewardship by managing well the resources their shareholders have entrusted to them.

Followers look to leaders for direction, and good stewards often have lofty purposes. A daily time of prayer followed by listening deeply for guidance through meditation is a good step toward thoughtful stewardship and true servant leadership.

Today's Journal

How has stewardship manifested itself in your leadership?

_____

_____

_____

_____

_____

_____

_____

_____

_____

_____

_____

_____

_____

_____

_____

_____

_____

Action Step – What one thing will you do today about these thoughts?

_____

_____

_____

_____

_____

SERVING

Take a moment to look back over your notes this week. Do your entries still resonate with you? Would you add anything?

And, how did you do on the actions steps you gave yourself? Be tough on yourself. If you didn't move on something, ask yourself why. And when you understand that "why", go just a little deeper and ask yourself again, why you want that outcome.

Comment here with additional thoughts and with whatever else you need to do about your notes and actions.

_____
_____
_____
_____
_____

Here are a few references on "serving" that might be helpful.

1) **"On Becoming a Servant Leader"** – Robert K. Greenleaf

2) **"The World's Most Powerful Leadership Principle – How to Become a Servant Leader"** – James C. Hunter

3) **"The Theology of the Hammer" – The Creation of Habitat for Humanity** – Millard Fuller

4) **"Reflections on Leadership – How the Theory of Servant-Leadership Influenced Today's Top Management Thinkers"** – Edited by Larry Spears

5) **"Trustees as Servants"** - Robert K. Greenleaf

6) **"Stewardship – Choosing Service Over Self-Interest"** – Peter Block

*"Leadership is expressing your talents
in the service of others."*

Kevin Cashman

CHAPTER TWELVE

"Love is eternal – the aspect may change, but not the essence.
And love makes one calmer about many things,
and that way, one is more fit for one's work."
Vincent van Gogh

LOVE

KEY PRINCIPLE THIS WEEK: LOVE

"Everybody can be great, because anybody can serve.
You don't have to have a college degree to serve.
You don't have to know about Plato and Aristotle to serve.
You don't have to know Einstein's Theory of Relativity to serve.
You only need a heart full of grace and a soul generated by love."

Martin Luther King

<u>Love</u>: *that quality in relationships which honors and appreciates others; the feeling of kindness or brotherhood toward others; an intense affection.*

To many leaders, the concept of love seems soft; but it can be very hard to love others.

Given how others can sometimes be angry or selfish, it's very challenging to not get caught up in that negativity. Using technology lingo, the November 2002 cover story of Fast Company magazine said "Love is the Killer App." The article stated, "compassion and empathy aren't management tools to be pulled out when needed; they're character traits most great leaders posses." [1]

To actually lead by example with love and compassion is more challenging than just powering over others. You've got to be well grounded, and a strong foundation in your spiritual practice can help. The biblical plea to "love your neighbor as yourself" starts with loving God and yourself. And scripture also says that loves contains nine component parts: patience, kindness, generosity, humility, courtesy, unselfishness, good temper, lack of suspicion and sincerity.

Love is the key to good relationships. And getting things done with and through others is central to leadership. As you'll see this week, love is about respect, openness, compassion, gratitude and caring. Most certainly the Golden Rule embodies love. Werner Erhard captured it uniquely when he wrote "you don't have to go looking for love when it's where you come from." [2]

I Choose Love…

To be compassionate toward others is my goal.
It's easy to talk about love, to promote loving others,
but for me it really starts with loving myself.
I need to learn how to better bring this principle
fully into my life and into my world.
As challenging as this might be, I choose love !

LOVE

LOVE YOUR GOD

"Love the Lord your God with all your heart and with all your soul and with all your mind. This is the first and greatest commandment. And the second is like it: Love your neighbor as yourself."

Matthew 22:37-38

Jesus was very clear with the Pharisees what was most important. It was about a relationship with the Creator that was complete and all encompassing. And the quality of that relationship was to be one of honor and awe – one of love.

For leaders, so much happens through other people. And we know that we can't force people to do things; we can't even demand compliance very effectively. People have to be willing to act for their efforts to be very useful. So the desired relationship with others needs to be respectful at a minimum, if not compassionate and appreciative. To the extent that a leader can move along the continuum toward love, imagine the potential that that quality can draw out of others.

Today's Journal

How would you describe your relationship with the Creator?

_____
_____
_____
_____
_____
_____
_____
_____
_____
_____
_____
_____
_____
_____
_____
_____
_____
_____
_____
_____
_____

Action Step – What one thing will you do today about these thoughts?

_____
_____
_____
_____
_____

LOVE

OPEN HEARTS

"Love opens hearts like knowledge opens mind."

Terces

Our worldly tendencies are to acquire knowledge, to get ahead and become street smart. And while these are generally worthy pursuits, they can become weapons to win at all costs.

Ethical leaders use their God-given intelligence for good purposes rather than to lord it over others. They find that loving others is a more effective approach because it builds relationships. And building up others is more powerful than an intellectual exercise any day.

Finding the right balance is difficult and critical to leadership. In his letter to the Corinthians, when St. Paul said that "knowledge puffs up, but love builds up" he was very perceptive about matters of the heart. And Terces quote here builds on this by putting the head and the heart more into balance.

Today's Journal

When do you allow knowledge to trump love?

_____
_____
_____
_____
_____
_____
_____
_____
_____
_____
_____
_____
_____
_____
_____
_____
_____
_____
_____
_____

Action Step – What one thing will you do today about these thoughts?

_____
_____
_____
_____
_____

LOVE

RECEIVE LOVE

> *"Only the open mind can receive wisdom;*
> *only the open heart can receive love."*
> **John Walsh Anglund**

The old adage that "it's better to give than to receive" is valid, but receiving the love of others is a gift in its own right. What does it mean to have an open heart?

An open heart is available to understand others' problems. It is receptive to their stories, both happy and sad. An open heart will accept an apology with grace and forgive unconditionally. But more than any of these characteristics, the ability to receive the love of another person signals a willingness to be in relationship. And relationships, not money, are what makes the world go 'round.

Leaders can really grow by being open. Powerful leaders learn to love and be loved.

Today's Journal

What do you see as the downside to an open heart and is it worth risking?

_____

_____

_____

_____

_____

_____

_____

_____

_____

_____

_____

_____

_____

_____

_____

_____

_____

_____

Action Step – What one thing will you do today about these thoughts?

_____

_____

_____

_____

_____

LOVE

EXPRESS GRATITUDE

*"You prepare a table before me in the presence of my enemies.
You anoint my head with oil; my cup overflows."*

Psalm 23: 5

The Almighty wants us to develop a habit of gratitude. He wants us to appreciate the blessings he has given us and to expand our capacity to receive more. The image that David painted with "my cup overflows" is a wonderful description of gratitude and a thankful heart full of love.

From a leadership perspective, gratitude is an attitude. It's a way of looking at everything as a gift from above. Being appreciative of our talents, our energy, our relationships, our resources, of everything really, is a function of an attitude of gratitude. And this attitude flows from loving relationships.

Today's Journal

How do you express gratitude?

_____

_____

_____

_____

_____

_____

_____

_____

_____

_____

_____

_____

_____

_____

_____

_____

_____

_____

Action Step – What one thing will you do today about these thoughts?

_____

_____

_____

_____

_____

LOVE

CARE ABOUT OTHERS

"People don't care how much you know,
until they know how much you care."

Stephen Covey

In the marketplace, it's really more about people and less about the product or the technology. Sure, the balance sheet tells a story, but without people, you can't build an enduring organization.

Covey's counsel here is more than a play on words because it's generally true. People can tell if you're interested in them. They can see it in your eyes and your body language. They want to know that you care and that their contributions are valued. It's just human nature.

Leaders who take a real interest in their people ask personal questions. About family. About health. About things that matter. And in doing so, they build relationships. You can be the smartest guy in the room, but if you don't connect with people, you won't go nearly as far.

Today's Journal

How do you show that you care?

_____

_____

_____

_____

_____

_____

_____

_____

_____

_____

_____

_____

_____

_____

_____

_____

_____

_____

Action Step – What one thing will you do today about these thoughts?

_____

_____

_____

_____

_____

LOVE

Take a moment to look back over your notes this week. Do your entries still resonate with you? Would you add anything?

And, how did you do on the actions steps you gave yourself? Be tough on yourself. If you didn't move on something, ask yourself why. And when you understand that "why", go just a little deeper and ask yourself again, why you want that outcome.

Comment here with additional thoughts and with whatever else you need to do about your notes and actions.

_____

_____

_____

_____

_____

Here are a few references on "love" that might be helpful.

1) **"The Leadership Bible: Leadership Principles from God's Word"** – Sid Buzzell, General Editor

2) **"Loving Monday"** – John Beckett

3) **"The Tao of Leadership"** – John Heider

4) **"Attitude is Everything – A Tune-up to Enhance Your Life"** – Keith Harrell

5) **"Love is the Killer App"** - Tim Sanders: Fast Company - November 2002

*"The values created by love
never fail"*

Walter Rauschenbusch

CHAPTER THIRTEEN

"First cleanse the inside…that the outside may be clean as well."
Matthew 23:26

SPIRITUALITY

KEY PRINCIPLE THIS WEEK: SPIRITUALITY

Rather than thinking of ourselves as humans having a spiritual experience,
think of yourself as a spiritual being having a human experience."
Wayne Dyer

Spirituality: *the process of honoring a presence greater than ourselves; an orientation toward God, the sacred or higher power, but not aligned with any specific religious belief.*

How is spirituality distinguished from religion? While some people use these terms interchangeably, there is actually a considerable difference.

Spirituality references God, but doesn't cross the line of how one relates to him. It's a process or state of mind – whereas religion is a way that that state of mind gets codified into rules. Spirituality is of the divine; religion is of man. Religion is institutional and is often about preserving that institution. And it's about doctrine, about having the right answer. So, spirituality and religion are related, but really different concepts.

Jon Meacham is his book <u>American Gospel</u>, claims that today spirituality is one of "the most pervasive but least understood forces in American life." [1] We need to make spiritual convictions a significant, but not the only or even dominant, factor in determining our political perspectives. It should be part of the process, not separate.

In Patricia Aburdene's book, "MegaTrends 2010 – The Rise of Conscious Capitalism" she describes why and how "the power of spirituality is arguably the greatest megatrend of our era." She claims that the "cornerstone of effective leadership is self-mastery" [2] and that this process of understanding "thyself" will often lead to getting beyond one's own selfish needs and recognizing a higher power.

But the divine presence has been gradually pushed out of our conversations over the past century. Our current materialistic culture advocates not just a separation of church and state, but a separation of church from life, where the Almighty has been restricted from the public square almost completely. On the contrary, it seems that with "In God We Trust," the nation's Founders intended to draw upon divine inspiration.

Today's media-driven culture tends to support "moral relativism" where all values are equal and the ends justify the means. But this approach is like quicksand that cannot serve as a foundation for anything. If change is needed, and if one rejects the ego-driven culture, then we need a powerful force greater than ourselves to make these changes. That influence can be spirituality.

When the Creator is introduced, we begin to get outside of ourselves, we get beyond our ego, and can begin to think about others – maybe even the common good. When God is present we tend to be more respectful, less irreverent; maybe even slightly vulnerable. When we bring the Almighty into the conversation, we're likely to get to the heart, and that's where values reside. At the heart level, we uncover our fundamentals – we hear what we really value and why. We get real. I like the proverb that says, "out of the overflow of the heart, the mouth speaks."

The encouraging news is that transcendent values, or spiritual values, are a common set of fundamental beliefs that are generally shared by the all world's great wisdom and faith traditions. All contain essentially the same truths. And when you compare spiritual values with more worldly values, you begin to see some striking differences.

God values humility over pride; pride being like a cancer on spirituality. He values encouragement and love over money and power. He values significance more than success. Spirituality tends to honor questions more than answers. Not knowing is appreciated, such that we don't always need to have the answer. Thinking about serving others versus being largely self-centered is common among the spiritually inclined.

The principle of spirituality is central to life and leadership. It represents a foundational element to how we make decisions and how we relate to others. The journaling here will cover selfishness, meaning, integration of head and heart, prayer and honoring everyone's perspective.

I Choose to be Spiritual

As I embark on this week,
I pray that divine inspiration will
guide my decisions and actions.
Give me patience to discern the right course.
Let my spiritual journey unfold!

SPIRITUALITY

GET BEYOND YOURSELF

> _"Spirituality is the process of living out a set of deeply held personal values, of honoring a presence greater than ourselves."_
> **Peter Block**

Perhaps one of the greatest leadership challenges today is excessive focus on the self. From self aggrandizement to pride to arrogance, for many, the ego has gotten out of control.

As Block raises the concept of a "presence greater than ourselves," it seems he's talking about a higher power, something beyond ourselves. Most people call that presence God, but other perfectly good references might be the divine, the Almighty, a transcendent force. Wayne Dyer uses the expression "source." The label is less important than the recognition of that greater life force.

For leaders, this concept is valuable because followers see pretty quickly when it's all about you. All kinds of things breakdown when selfishness prevails. So, to recognize that you are not the only one is a huge first step. This notion is at the core of spirituality.

Today's Journal

Who or what is at the center of your life?

_____

_____

_____

_____

_____

_____

_____

_____

_____

_____

_____

_____

_____

_____

_____

_____

_____

_____

Action Step – What one thing will you do today about these thoughts?

_____

_____

_____

_____

_____

SPIRITUALITY

SEEK MEANING

> _"Genuine spirituality is the willingness to enter into a process of dialogue_
> _about meaning, within oneself and with others_
> _and to stay with it over a period of time."_
> **Peter Vaill**

This reference to spirituality is born out of the concept of questions rather than answers. Because things divine are often a mystery, the process of discovery is an inquiry. Religions contend they have the answer...sometimes all the answers. Most people call this dogma. But, the truth is no one has all the answers - at least not down here on earth.

Many of the best leaders are seekers. As Vaill contends, to seek meaning takes time, and often it's a life-long process. Whether it's a deep question about the meaning of life, or simply an issue of strategy, seeking to understand through an open dialogue expands one's perspective. Leaders are seekers who attract others. On the contrary, most people don't like to hang-out with a know-it-all.

Today's Journal

How have you gone about the search for meaning?

_____

_____

_____

_____

_____

_____

_____

_____

_____

_____

_____

_____

_____

_____

_____

_____

_____

_____

Action Step – What one thing will you do today about these thoughts?

_____

_____

_____

_____

_____

SPIRITUALITY

INTEGRATE HEAD WITH HEART

> *"I use the word heart as they did in ancient times,*
> *when it didn't merely mean the emotions,*
> *as it tends to mean today. It meant that center in the human*
> *self where everything comes together –*
> *where will and intellect and values and feeling and intuition and vision all converge.*
> *It meant the source of one's integrity. It takes courage to lead from the heart."*
>
> ### Parker Palmer

Palmer's definition of heart is wonderfully comprehensive. It implies the power of the spiritual that can bring all of these elements together. Spirituality causes integration.

Effective, ethical leaders need to draw upon both head and heart. The Creator gave us free will to choose and yet reminds us periodically that he's got a plan too. So, the integration of paradoxes - the analytical with the gut, a strategy with compassion, action laced with patience – is a key leadership process. But in the final analysis, if you find conflict between these extremes, follow your heart.

Today's Journal

Describe a situation where you found your head and heart in conflict. What did you do?

_____

_____

_____

_____

_____

_____

_____

_____

_____

_____

_____

_____

_____

_____

_____

_____

_____

_____

_____

_____

Action Step – What one thing will you do today about these thoughts?

_____

_____

_____

_____

_____

SPIRITUALITY

RENEW THROUGH PRAYER AND MEDITATION

"Love begins at home, in your own family, and it begins by praying together.
Prayer gives a clean heart, and a clean heart can see God. And if you see
God in each other, you will have love, peace and joy together.
And works of love are works of peace. And love begins at home."

Mother Teresa

What a powerful reminder – that loves begins at home. This is no complex theory needing testing and analysis. It's simple common sense. Love is connected to God and we connect to him through prayer and meditation.

True, but what's this got to do with leadership? Much like the strength of family ties, a strong organization is likely to be made up of people who care about one another. When you have relationships of trust, better results will be produced. Leaders can usually see more clearly when they take a few moments to reflect, to pray for guidance before an important meeting or decision. And then taking just a bit longer to listen – to meditate - can rejuvenate one's thinking and one's spirit !

Today's Journal

When is the last time you had a prayer answered?

_____
_____
_____
_____
_____
_____
_____
_____
_____
_____
_____
_____
_____
_____
_____
_____
_____
_____
_____

Action Step – What one thing will you do today about these thoughts?

_____
_____
_____
_____
_____

SPIRITUALITY

HONOR THE FAITH OF EACH PERSON

> *"We cannot escape the necessity of love and compassion.*
> *This, then is my true religion, my simple faith.*
> *In this sense, there is no need for temple or church, for mosque or synagogue,*
> *no need for complicated philosophy, doctrine or dogma.*
> *Our own heart, our mind, is the temple.*
> *The doctrine is compassion. Love for others and respect for their rights and dignity,*
> *no matter who or what they are."*
>
> **Dali Lama**

This speaks to how spirituality differs from religion. The spirit is not tied to a set of rules, but rather about the set of your heart. What is needed is not dogma, but an open heart ready to both give and receive.

In leadership, it's the same. Honor the other guy's spiritual perspective. Look for the common ground and you will find that the Dali Lama is right. If you love the other guy first, most everything else will fall in place. In his book <u>American Gospel</u>, Jon Meacham agrees when he says, "A reverence for one's own tradition is not incompatible with respect for the tradition of others." [3]   It's all about love.

Today's Journal

What holds you back from honoring the other guy?

_____
_____
_____
_____
_____
_____
_____
_____
_____
_____
_____
_____
_____
_____
_____
_____
_____
_____

Action Step – What one thing will you do today about these thoughts?

_____
_____
_____
_____
_____

SPIRITUALITY

Take a moment to look back over your notes this week. Do your entries still resonate with you? Would you add anything?

And, how did you do on the actions steps you gave yourself? Be tough on yourself. If you didn't move on something, ask yourself why. And when you understand that "why", go just a little deeper and ask yourself again, why you want that outcome.

Comment here with additional thoughts and with whatever else you need to do about your notes and actions.

_____

_____

_____

_____

_____

Here are a few references on "spirituality" that might be helpful.

1) **"Man's Search for Meaning"** – Viktor Frankl
2) **"MegaTrends – 2010"** – Patricia Aburdene
3) **"The Road Less Traveled"** – Scott Peck
4) **"The Reinvention of Work"** – Matthew Fox
5) **"The Tao of Leadership"** – John Heider
6) **"Encouraging the Heart"** – James Kouzes & Barry Posner

*"Create in me a clean heart, O God,
and renew a steadfast spirit within me."*

Psalm 51:10

LETTER TO MY FAMILY

I wanted each of you to know how both your presence in my life, together with God's word, has deeply influenced my leadership. But I just wanted to say it more directly than I have over the years.

Leadership can be a complex subject. There are so many facets and characteristics and virtues; the list could just go on and on. I have always admired those who have kept their message simple and clear in the face of complexity. That's why I was drawn to the Bible, and particularly to Jesus' words, to make my approach known on leadership.

How did I come to this? First, my heart goes out to our mother. It was her perseverance and steadfastness that took us to the Central Northwest Presbyterian Church in Detroit. Here Pastor Tommy Higgins planted the seed. But I give the credit to Mom!

It flowered one night as a teenager when Billy Graham made his alter call and I accepted the offer. But my faith lay relatively dormant for years through college and Vietnam and even through the early years of marriage. Pam and I usually attended services at Christmas and Easter, but it was a tepid faith for sure.

And then came the children. As parents, we just knew that we had to re-introduce faith into our family to provide that solid foundation that Jesus called "the rock." When I discovered Brooke's hand-written poster declaring that it was in Erica Pedone's sixth grade class that "God had come into her life" it hit me like a ton of bricks. Here was faith right in my own home and I was still wandering around out there. It was a wake-up call!

Then, just a few years later, I learned what a "divine call" was like. When our pastor, Dan Rolhwing, announced plans to build a Christian high school, I received a tap on my shoulder, at least it felt like that, about leading this effort. Before long, I was chairing the Board of Trustees, and Conor enrolled in the first class. As my faith began to unfold at Vail Christian, I started to read the Bible again. It was Sid

213

Buzzell's editing of the "Leadership Bible" that brought God's word and leadership principles into alignment for me. And later, Ken Blanchard's recommendation to "lead like Jesus," really captured my attention and helped me see the beauty of his leadership approach and the resulting movement he spawned.

And then September 11th hit. Out of this tragedy, Pam started a prayer group that has been meeting every Wednesday ever since. Her focus on prayer and all the aspects of this heart-felt practice have brought our family closer together, even if they don't all recognize it yet.

This book, which contains a lifetime of my thinking, is dedicated to all of you for your role in helping me to grow in my faith. I just wish I had gotten serious about divine inspiration earlier. The Almighty has blessed me with a wonderful family and I am thankful !

I love you all !

JHK

P.S. Here's a little prayer that I often use to begin the week...

"Father God,
thank you for the blessings of this life
and for nourishing me on my journey.
I pray that your word will touch my heart, Lord,
and that your Holy Spirit will guide my plans
and leadership actions this week.
Help me, Lord, to understand your will for my life
that I might more fully serve you and those around me.
Help me to frequently ask; 'What would Jesus do?'

I pray this in your holy name, Amen."

Chapter Notes

INTRODUCTION

[1] The Leader Within; Ken Blanchard

[2] The Purpose Driven Life; Rick Warren

[3] The Seven Habits of Highly Effective People; Stephen R. Covey

CHAPTER ONE – THE EVOLUTION OF A LEADERSHIP PERSPECTIVE

[1] Leader to Leader; Leadership and the Inner Journey; Fall 2001

[2] A Hidden Wholeness; Parker Palmer

[3] The Seven Habits of Highly Effective People; Stephen R. Covey

[4] The Leadership Bible; Matthew 23:26

[5] What Color is a Conservative; J.C. Watts

[6] A Hidden Wholeness; Parker Palmer

[7] Synchronicity: The Inner Path of Leadership; Joseph Jaworski

[8] Fast Company Magazine; November 2002

[9] Stewardship: Choosing Service Over Self-Interest; Peter Block

[10] The Re-Invention of Work; Matthew Fox

[11] The Purpose Driven Life; Rick Warren

CHAPTER TWO – VALUES: BUILDING BLOCKS FOR LEADERS

[1] Seven Habits of Highly Effective People; Stephen Covey

[2] True North; Bill George

[3] Spirituality of Leadership; Bill Grace

[4] Being the Body; Chuck Colson

CHAPTER THREE – PURPOSE

[1] Power of Purpose; Richard Leider

[2] Ibid

CHAPTER FOUR – INTEGRITY

[1] What Color is a Conservative; J.C. Watts

[2] Ethics 101; John Maxwell

CHAPTER SIX - ATTITUDE

[1] General Douglas MacArthur

[2] George Bernard Shaw

CHAPTER SEVEN – VISIONING

[1] Visionary Leadership; Burt Nanus

[2] Lead Like Jesus; John Ortberg

[3] Seven Habits of Highly Effective People; Stephen Covey

[4] Ibid

[5] Good to Great; Jim Collins

CHAPTER EIGHT - COMMUNICATING

[1] Seven Habits of Highly Effective People; Stephen Covey

CHAPTER NINE – LEARNING

[1] LifeLaunch; Frederic Hudson

CHAPTER TEN – EXECUTING

[1] Seven Habits of Highly Effective People; Stephen Covey

CHAPTER ELEVEN – SERVING

[1] On Becoming a Servant Leader; Robert K. Greenleaf

[2] Seven Habits of Highly Effective People; Stephen Covey

[3] George Bernard Shaw

[4] Seven Habits of Highly Effective People; Stephen Covey

CHAPTER TWELVE - LOVE

[1] Love is the Killer App; Fast Company; November 2002

[2] Aphorisms; Werner Erhard; 1973

CHAPTER THIRTEEN - SPIRITUALITY

[1] <u>American Gospel</u>; Jon Meacham

[2] <u>MegaTrends 2010</u>; Patricia Aburdene

[3] <u>American Gospel</u>; Jon Meacham

LEARNING GROUPS

While this journal was originally conceived for individual use, it can also serve as a group learning tool. By coming together in small groups of 5 to 6 to discuss your leadership perspectives, a powerful growth opportunity can be available.

The purpose of these groups is simple – it's about learning from each other. When we have close, trusting relationships where we can talk about matters that are important – matters of the heart – we benefit from the wisdom of others. We realize fairly quickly that others have learned similar lessons as you, and they have similar problems and similar hopes and dreams.

Small learning groups have been meeting for centuries, if not millennia, in many forms. In his book, <u>Power of Purpose</u>, Richard Leider sites Benjamin Franklin as the founder of the "Junto" that met weekly on issues of morals and politics. Parker Palmer in his book, <u>A Hidden Wholeness</u>, promotes "Circles of Trust" and many faith organizations promote "accountability groups." Regardless of name or focus, these types of groups allow us to share our perspectives, get advice and council and build lasting relationships.

How to get started?

- Ask a handful of friends or colleagues to acquaint themselves with this book and then come together for a coffee or lunch. Talk about your interests and needs and how you want to come together on a periodic basis.
- If the group decides on a weekly schedule, then use the flow of the journaling chapters as the focal point of your gatherings. Use any of the questions posed each day to guide your dialogue. Or ask what did you discover as you worked through each day? What surprised you?
- If monthly seems more appropriate, then organize your discussions around the four major parts, or realms, of the book – Foundations, Character, Skills and Relationships. Whatever

your timeframe, secure commitments from each person to meet regularly. Set aside at least 1 ½ hours for these gatherings. Be reasonable and practical, but be committed.

- Choose a private location like someone's study or library. Avoid public spaces as these will cause interruptions to break the flow of your dialogue. Some groups like to rotate the meeting place, but experience shows that a consistent place allows for more productive use of the time. Some groups like to designate a leader each session, while others prefer a more open approach.
- As you conclude your review of the journal, pose the question to the group – should we continue to meet like this. If so, what will be your new focus?

"It is our commitment to the conversation itself - our willingness to put forward our observations and interpretations for testing by the community and to return the favor to others. To be in the truth, we must know how to observe and reflect and speak and listen, with passion and with discipline."

Parker Palmer

ABOUT THE AUTHOR

John Horan-Kates has over 35 years of leadership experience in business and community organizations. He received an undergraduate degree in business from Wayne State University in Detroit in 1967 and subsequently became a Distinguished Naval Graduate of the U.S. Navy's Officer Candidate School. Following this training, he served aboard the USS Jennings County in Vietnam.

*After departing the Navy in 1972, he served as Controller for the Kirkwood Resort in the California High Sierra. Several years later he came to Vail and served as Vice-President of Marketing for **Vail Resorts**, founded the **Vail Valley Foundation**, helped build the **Vilar Center for the Arts** and then helped start **Vail Christian High School**. In 1997, he helped launched the **Vail Leadership Institute** where he continues to serve as President.*

*In 1998, he received a Master Coaching Certificate from the **Hudson Institute of Santa Barbara**. He is the author of several leadership essays and has published two leadership guidebooks.*

He has lived in Colorado's Vail Valley with his wife Pam since 1974. They have two children living and working in Boulder, Colorado.